50 Ways to Paint Furniture

The Easy Step-by-Step Way to Decorator Looks

Elise C. Kinkead

Creative Publishing
international
Chanhassen, Minnesota

This book is dedicated to those who have taught me.

Elise C. Kinkead

Copyright 2007
Creative Publishing international
18705 Lake Drive East
Chanhassen, Minnesota 55317
1-800-328-3895
www.creativepub.com
All rights reserved

**Creative Publishing
international**

President/CEO: Ken Fund

50 WAYS TO PAINT FURNITURE

Executive Managing Editor: Barbara Harold

Development Editor: Sharon Boerbon Hanson

Photo Stylist: Joanne Wawra

Creative Director: Michele Lanci-Altomare

Photographers: Rudy Calin, Steve Galvin, Andrea Rugg

Production Manager: Laura Hokkanen

Cover and Book Design: Brad Springer

Page Layout: Lois Stanfield

Library of Congress Cataloging-in-Publication Data

Kinkead, Elise C.
  50 ways to paint furniture: the easy, step-by-step way
to decorator looks / Elise C. Kinkead.
       p. cm.
  ISBN-13: 978-1-58923-292-1 (soft cover)
  ISBN-10: 1-58923-292-5 (soft cover)
  1. Furniture painting. 2. Finishes and finishing. I.
Title.

  TT199.4.K56 2007
  745.7'23--dc22
2006032897

Printed in China
10 9 8 7 6 5 4 3 2 1

Contents

Creating Your Style

YOU DON'T HAVE the heart to get rid of Grandma's old table. What do you do with it? You've changed the bedroom carpet and now your favorite bedside tables look out of place.

Paint them!

50 Ways to Paint Furniture offers creative ways to revamp furniture, stirs the imagination, and inspires you to give new life to tired old furniture pieces or create a masterpiece on a fresh "canvas." It supplies you with techniques to complete a wide variety of furniture finishes—with sensational results. These foundational techniques form the basis on which you can lay your imagination.

As you delve into this wonderful world of decoration, keep in mind this very important point: *50 Ways to Paint Furniture* contains technical information. You, the craftsperson, provide the creativity. Give yourself the aesthetic permission to explore, to imagine, and to realize that you *can* render beautiful work. Your inspiration will then be true and accurate. The desire to produce an intriguing piece of art (for that is what your furniture becomes) is an ancient yearning. This book will help you satisfy that urge.

When you select your finish, open your paints, and roll up your sleeves, you start a creative process. You are the artist. So allow your self-expression to come forward. Allow yourself to create what you find desirable.

There are no rules, only compatibilities. Does this finish work with this piece? Does this paint work with that paint? What if I did this, what if I try that, and what if I purposely put two incompatibles together?

While striving for beauty and elegance, accept that you are not a machine. Your personality, in combination with that of the furniture piece, will work together to create a harmonious and graceful result. You are the one to satisfy. Use the techniques outlined in the following pages to please yourself. How do you know when a piece of furniture or a finish is done? When you like it!

Go forth—bravely and boldly—but relaxed. Enjoy the process as your hands produce. Satisfy your desire to bring a bit of beauty into your home for the enjoyment of all. Use the techniques outlined in this book as a springboard—a suggestion—to create a furniture piece that you will be proud of, amused by, intrigued with, and that will enhance your home.

It's a wonderful journey. Have fun along the way and your enjoyment will be reflected in your final result.

Secrets to Discover Before You Begin

THE PROJECT PAGES contain techniques; they're like flowers, full of beauty. The pages in *Secrets to Know Before You Begin*, as well as *All About ...*, and *Basic Techniques* contain upfront knowledge; they're like garden soil—how fertile (or good) it is determines the success of the flowers. Reading them will make all the difference.

Step Zero

Every time an artist, a craftsperson, or a do-it-yourselfer starts a project, the aim is the same: SUCCESS. There is a secret to achieving that—always start at Step Zero.

Starting at Step Zero means reading all pertinent sections of *Before You Begin* and then reading through the project instructions *before* starting to paint. *50 Ways to Paint Furniture* suggests you buy high-quality equipment for the best project outcome. Being fully prepared by equipping yourself with knowledge and proper tools and materials helps you create the great finish you want.

The Base of Success

The success of the basecoat dictates the success of the finish. Before basecoating a previously stained or painted surface, refer to *Cleaning* on page 16. Unless otherwise specified, apply painted basecoats with a 5" (12.7 cm) foam roller. Allow the paint to dry; then sand with 220-grit sandpaper. Remove the sanding dust with a tack cloth.

Equipment

The instructions for all finishes in *50 Ways to Paint Furniture* assume you have a basic painting kit when you begin a project. Always buy high-quality tools and materials (both for your kit and for your project supplies), as they help you achieve the best results.

- 220-grit sandpaper (used whenever a grit is not specified in the materials list)
- 400- and 600-grit wet/dry sandpaper
- tack cloths to remove sanding dust and to prepare the surface for topcoating
- drop cloths to protect work area floors
- stir sticks for mixing
- empty paint containers (with lids) for mixing and dirty rag disposal
- foam roller, 5" (12.7 cm)
- roller handle to use with the roller
- paint tray
- dust masks
- gloves
- safety glasses
- blue painter's tape*
- craft knife*
- tape machine (this makes taping a breeze)

*Sizes of painter's tape vary and there are many good craft knifes available; these items are not shown.

All About...

PAINTS, STAINS, glazes, topcoats, colorant, wax—the world of furniture finishes is full of products, procedures, and painterly terms. This section explains them, so you can make the best choices when choosing supplies for your project.

All About Paints

Paints offer versatility in color, composition, and opacity. They bring finishes to life or serve as a base for glazes.

Latex

Buy latex paint from a paint store, not a craft store; it's less expensive and comes in larger containers. It comes in four sheens: flat, very dull when dry; eggshell, very low sheen; semi-gloss, and gloss. Eggshell, semi-gloss, and gloss are poor choices for the techniques in *50 Ways to Paint Furniture* as they are too "slippery."

Oil-based

Oil-based paint is also purchased at a paint or home store and available in the same four sheen levels. Oil-based eggshell sheen is called "low luster." Low luster is the only sheen used in the techniques, although gloss is recommended as a topcoat on some finishes.

Japan Color

This is a super finely ground color pigment mixed with a drying agent. An oil-based paint, it comes premixed in small containers and is available in a wide variety of colors. Japan Color paint dries completely flat and is desirable owing to the radiance of its colors. Japan Colors can be found online or at good woodworking stores.

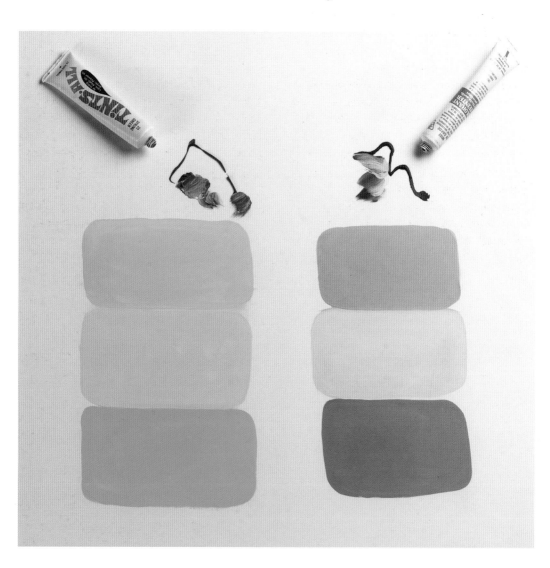

Artist Tube Paints

Either acrylic or oil-based tube paints can be used when you need only a small amount of a color. They cost more per ounce than any other paint. If you use artist oils, mix two- or three-parts paint with one-part alkyd glazing liquid and a small amount of mineral spirits to promote drying.

Milk Paint

This paint is also called casein paint. It is truly milk-based. Milk paint comes as a dry powder to be mixed with water. It's very good for cer-tain finishes, but is the weakest and least dur-able of all the paints.

Universal Tinting Colorant (UTC)

UTC is not paint, but an additive used to tint all types of paint. In fact, it's used in the machine at the paint store to color paint. UTC comes in small tubes or pint sizes; buy the smallest tube, as it is a very powerful color agent. In addition to tinting paint, it also tints varnishes. UTCs never dry on their own, so wipe up spills quick-ly or the UTC will spread over everything. UTCs are transparent until added to paint.

All About Product Compatibility

Latex (water-based) paint may be put over any latex product but not over an oil-based product. Water is the solvent for latex products, and is used to remove or thin the paint.

Oil-based paints may be put over oil-based and latex products. Mineral spirits or paint thin-ner are the solvents for oil-based products, and are used to remove or thin the paint.

Acrylic-based varnishes may be applied over latex products. Oil-based varnishes may be applied over oil-based and latex products. Lower-sheen varnishes go over higher-sheen varnishes as the higher the sheen, the stronger the varnish. It is common to apply the first var-nish coat in a gloss and then the sheen of choice.

Polishing waxes may be applied over latex or oil-based products.

Caution: Although there are a number of good spray varnishes and topcoats on the market, some of these may be incompatible with certain paints and cause lifting or cracking (called craz-ing). Always ask at the paint store if a spray product may be applied over your paint. An incompatibility could destroy your work. Never use spray lacquers as they are dangerous to your health and the environment.

All About Glazes

A glaze is paint thinned to a slightly transparent quality and the consistency of whole milk. The binding agent in paint loses strength when thinned with a solvent, but glazing liquid restores strength to paint. Glazing liquid is clear, flat, and does not affect the color of the paint.

Varnish tinted with a small amount of paint also acts as a glaze. UTC may be used to tint a varnish for a very transparent glaze.

The basic recipe for a latex paint glaze is one-part paint, one-part acrylic glazing liquid, and one-part water. Add the water slowly to avoid thinning the glaze too far (add more paint and glazing liquid if this occurs). If the glaze appears too thick, add more water.

The basic recipe for an oil glaze is one-part paint, one-part alkyd glazing liquid, and two-parts mineral spirits. Add the mineral spirits slowly to avoid thinning the glaze too far (add more paint and glazing liquid if this occurs). If the glaze appears too thick, add more mineral spirits.

Many standard glazes are used with the finishes in *50 Ways to Paint Furniture*. Two fun variations are tinted oil-based varnish and stained overglaze.

Tinted Oil Varnish

Tint oil varnish slightly with UTC burnt umber and UTC raw umber. Apply using a paintbrush or foam roller. This offers a lovely, slightly aged transparent quality.

Stained Overglaze

For oil-based paints, mix one-part paint, one-part alkyd glazing liquid, and eight-parts mineral spirits. For latex paints, mix one-part paint, one-part acrylic glazing liquid, and eight-parts water. Apply using a paintbrush or foam roller. The glaze will be skim milk consistency. Overglazes help reduce contrast and also add translucent beauty to surfaces.

All About Stains

Use stains to add color to wood. There are many colors and types, and compatible types may be mixed to make custom colors. Whatever type of stain you choose, wipe it on with one lint-free T-shirt rag and wipe it off with a clean one.

Gel Stain
Full-bodied gel stains are easy to work with and can be used as an overglaze right from the can. Find them in paint stores. In the top example, a red mahogany was applied over birch wood.

Pure Color Stain
Pure color stains come in vivid colors. Find them at woodworkers' stores. In the middle example, a bright cheerful green was applied over birch wood.

Japan Color
Mix the Japan Color to a skim milk consistency with mineral sprits; wipe it on and then immediately wipe off the project surface. Unlike gels or pure color stains, paint-based Japan Color is compatible with all oil paints, so any oil paint may easily be applied over it. In the bottom example, a Prussian blue was applied over birch wood.

Safety Procedures
Always wear safety glasses, dust masks, and gloves, as necessary, to protect yourself when sanding and working with paints and solvents. Always read manufacturer's instructions for proper cleanup and disposal information. Always work in well-ventilated areas to avoid build-up of fumes.

Safety Caution
Stains and rags used for staining are combustible. Linseed oil (found in most staining materials) causes them to give off heat as they dry, enabling them to self-combust. *Never* throw a dirty staining rag in your trash. Fill an empty gallon-size paint container with water. When finished staining, immerse the rags in the water and tightly seal the lids. Dispose of the materials properly.

All About Topcoats

"Topcoat" refers to any medium that protects a furniture surface. Varnish and wax are used on the projects in *50 Ways to Paint Furniture as* they are good topcoats and the easiest to apply.

Varnish

Oil-based varnishes tend to level out (flow together) better than water-base varnishes, and they offer a richer appearance. Never apply a water-based varnish over an oil-based varnish.

Always use the highest quality paintbrush possible to apply varnish, and keep that paintbrush exclusively for varnishing. Load your brush with roughly 1" (1.3 cm) of varnish, and lay-off (apply) quickly, always ending in a full top-to-bottom or side-to-side stroke and continuing until the project surface is evenly coated. Never over-brush varnish; it will set too quickly and refuse to level out. Good varnishing takes practice and the more you do it, the better you will become.

Do not thin varnish. You may gently heat oil varnish to help it level out. Put the amount you need in a clean container. Set the container in a pot of *previously* boiled water.

The higher the gloss level, the stronger a varnish dries. Apply a gloss varnish as the first topcoat; then apply subsequent layers in the sheen of choice. Lightly wet-sand the dry gloss varnish with 400-grit wet/dry sandpaper before applying a lower sheen. The three sheen levels (shown in the top example) for either oil-based or water-based varnishes are gloss, satin, and dull/flat.

Wax

Wax gives a beautiful hand-rubbed gleam to surfaces. Paste wax with a high carnauba content produces a very strong finish. The example shown is a pecan-stained pine board finished with three coats of paste wax.

Basic Techniques

THE PROPER PREPARATION of surfaces, how to do the various brush manipulation techniques, and all the tools, techniques, and tricks are in this helpful section. Reading about the techniques may inspire you to try your hand at one of finishes that looks difficult, but is deceptively simple.

Basecoat Techniques

A good basecoat takes a finish from okay to "oh-my-gosh" extraordinary.

Cleaning

This is the simplest of all the basecoats. Clean the entire furniture piece with denatured alcohol using #000 steel wool; then wipe the entire surface with a lint-free rag and denatured alcohol. Sand with 150-grit sandpaper and wipe again. The denatured alcohol will remove old wax, polishing product residue, grease, and grime. If a furniture piece requires stripping of layers of stain or paint, refer to the manufacturer's instructions for any product you choose to use.

Priming

If you will be painting on raw wood, or if the surface is already painted with an unknown type of paint, repaint the surface with a primer. A good primer seals the surface, covers undesirable stains, stops bleed-through, and prevents paint adhesion problems.

Primers come in latex and oil-based formulas, but use acrylic bonding primer as it is better for the environment and for you. For small pieces such as chairs and for carved items such as picture or mirror frames, spray primers are a sensible choice.

Brushing

On the example shown, primer is being applied with a 2" (5.1 cm) angled-edge latex paintbrush. Paint the interior of an inset before other areas, and always follow the grain of the wood when applying primer. Be as neat as if applying a finish paint coat.

Rolling

If the area is large or you are unsure of your brushing ability, use a combination of brushing and rolling. First, brush primer neatly into recesses, corners, and edges, and then using a 5" (12.7) foam roller, apply primer to the remaining surface.

Avoid overloading the foam roller. Load the foam roller in the roller tray; then roll off some of the primer on scrap wood or in a clean area of the tray. It's best to apply a thin coat of primer on your project surface. The beauty of using a foam roller is it leaves very little "roller stipple." Keep rolling the primer, with a light pressure, until you have a very smooth application with low roller stipple. Practice loading and rolling, as it will save you irritation when priming large surfaces.

Spraying

Zinsser B-I-N® is a white shellac-based primer. It is an extremely effective sealant for most surfaces and may be sprayed on. Follow the manufacturer's label instructions.

Tip: Shellac-based products are alcohol based. If you get a big drip or paint sag, allow it to dry, then rub it smooth with a little denatured alcohol. Most sags and drips flatten on their own.

Painting Techniques

These are the methods of removing, adding, or manipulating paints and glazes used in *50 Ways to Paint Furniture*.

Tufbacking

Tufbacking is also known as wet sanding. The technique works best on oil-based paints and sprayed enamels.

This technique takes a surface from nice to knockout. Tufback after the final oil-based paint basecoat, after the final basecoat before gilding, and after the second-to-last coat of varnish.

After the final coat of paint or varnish is dry, spray a workable area of the project surface with water using a spray bottle. Use 400-grit wet/dry sandpaper, and sand using a small circular motion. Wipe the water off frequently with paper towels to check your progress. Be patient; there is no way to hurry this process. Do the final sanding with the 600-grit wet/dry sandpaper. When are you done? Dry the surface and look at it sideways and on an angle. The surface should have an even sheen and be as smooth as glass.

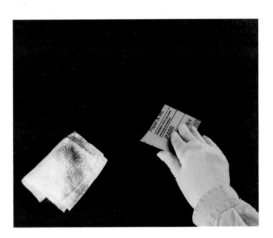

Laying Off

There is a proper stroking method to achieve an even coat of paint. Use short up-and-down, then back-and-forth strokes, ending with one soft, long pull end to end. This evenly distributes the paint, producing a smooth paint layer. This needs to be done quickly to allow the wet paint areas to blend together readily.

Blending

After applying a coat of oil-based paint, but before it sets up, use a dry oil paintbrush to gently brush in a crosshatch pattern over the top of the paint. This softly blends the paint and knocks down paintbrush ridges.

Dry Brush

Pick up a small amount of paint evenly across the bristle tips of a flat paintbrush. Pat the bristles on a dry paper towel or clean rag to off-load the paint. Pull the paintbrush across the project surface using a light pressure.

French Brush

This technique spreads the paint over the surface quickly with total coverage. Apply the paint in a criss-cross fashion, arcing in and around and ending with an upstroke off the surface. Use either a straight or angled-edge paintbrush.

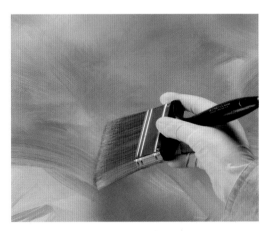

Pouncing

Apply glaze using the French brush technique and while it's wet, tap perpendicularly on the surface with a 2" (5.1 cm) oval sash paintbrush using moderate pressure. This technique gives you a very tight "dotted" surface. The end result should look even, but a slight variation here and

there is okay. This is a good way to blend two colors together.

Folding

To fold a glaze means to soften the texture and to reduce contrast and pattern, usually with a cheesecloth wad.

Using Cheesecloth

The example shown below is the appropriate shape of a 90-weight cheesecloth wad. The side that touches the paint surface is fairly smooth, without wrinkles or little tails.

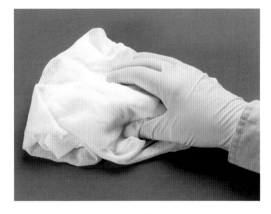

Distressing and Aging: Techniques and Tools

Distressing a surface means to physically mar it to suggest the wear and tear of age. To distress paint means making it appear rubbed off or worn away. Physical distressing can be a lot of fun.

Hammer

You simply pound the surface. Wear will happen in predictable places, so examine the furniture piece to decide where wear might have occurred. Then go for it!

Nail

Lay a nail on its side and pound the nail head with a hammer. Create small holes by pounding only the point of the nail into the project surface. Press and drag a nail along the surface to make a deep scratch.

Chisel

Use a wood chisel to make factory-fresh surfaces look like they've been around for a while. Carve off corners and crisp edges, and gouge deep into the surface for extreme wear.

Sandpaper

Use 100-grit sandpaper to pull paint off edges and corners revealing the wood underneath. Sand paint off larger areas to simulate wear. A bonus to using sandpaper to distress is that you have also sanded the surface smooth.

Antiquing: Positive Method

To antique a surface using the positive method means to apply paint, varnish, or stain, to suggest age.

When you antique, allow the antiquing glaze to remain heavier in the corners and the recesses of the surface where dirt and dust would normally build up. Apply the antiquing glaze with a paintbrush, wipe the surface with a soft lint-free T-shirt rag, and then softly blend with a clean paintbrush to remove obvious brushstrokes.

In the example shown, a warm, almost dusty, colored gray glaze was applied over a red basecoat.

Antiquing: Negative Method

Antiquing with the negative method means to remove paint—it simulates wear that rubbed the paint down to the base over years of use.

To remove oil paint, use sandpaper. To remove latex paint, dip a T-shirt rag into denatured alcohol and rub the area where you want to remove the paint, using both circular and up-and-down motions. A believable and soft aging occurs with no need for sanding.

In the example shown, a coat of flat blue latex was applied over a primer coat and allowed to dry. Denatured alcohol was then used to remove the paint in logical "wear" areas.

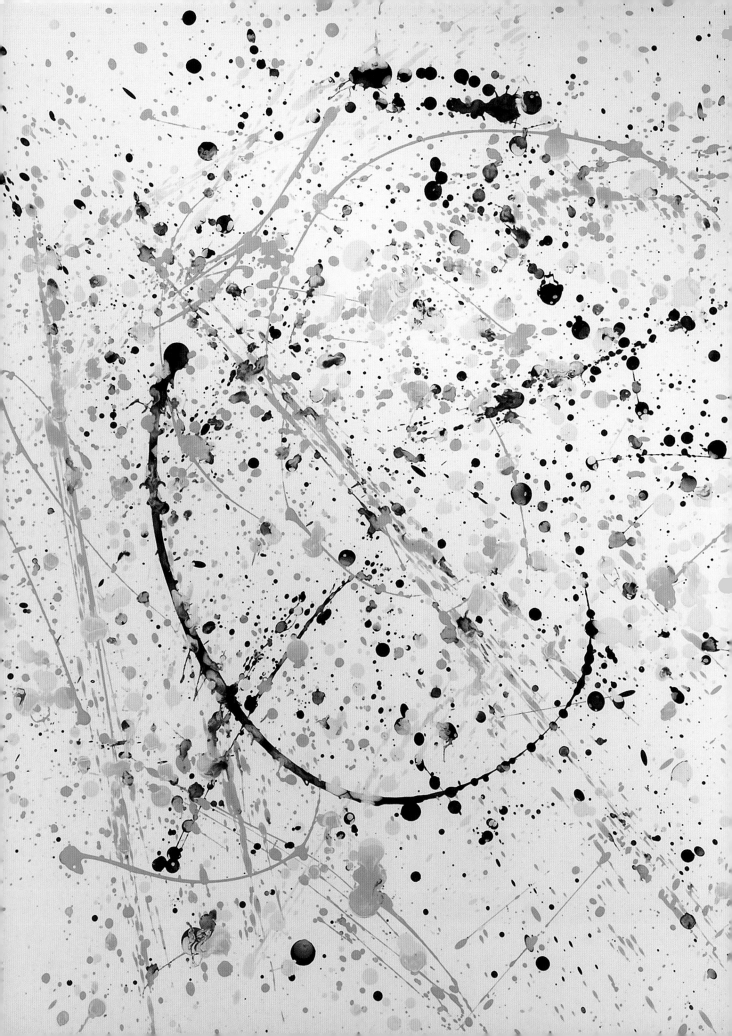

Creative PAINT EFFECTS

THIS ELEGANT FINISH reproduces the lacquerware techniques used by Japanese monks since the fourteenth century. They first applied a black lacquer basecoat followed by a red lacquer coat. As the objects were used, the red wore away revealing the black underneath. The *Negoro Nuri* finish requires a bit of patience, restraint, and thoughtfulness but the dramatic result is very rewarding.

For best results, choose furniture with straight lines and objects of simple design. Study your furniture piece and imagine where the natural wear patterns will be. Edges, corners, legs, and tops are the most common. The appearance will be most believable and graceful if the wear pattern is asymmetrical.

1 Negoro Nuri

Pick a bright red with a slight orangey undertone. The traditional colors of this finish are red over black, but experiment if you're a rebel.

Because the finish is achieved by "tufbacking" (page 18), it is necessary to use oil-based paints. Numerous coats of the black and the red also must be evenly applied, with overnight drying times. This is where the patience comes in. Take your time and enjoy watching the finish emerge.

Refer to *Tufbacking* (page 18), and pages 7, 8, 14, and 16 to 19 before beginning.

- flat/matte oil-based or spray paint, black
- flat* oil-based paint, red/orange

*satin may be substituted if necessary

- mineral spirits
- flat oil paintbrush, 3" (7.6 cm)
- paper towels or clean rags

- spray bottle
- wet/dry sandpaper, 400- and 600-grit
- gloss oil-based varnish

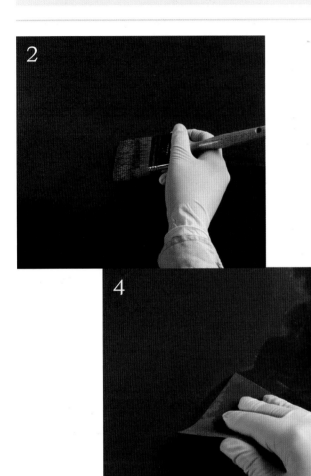

1 Basecoat the project surface with three coats of black paint using the paintbrush, or spray paint applied carefully in very thin coats. Avoid sags and drips. Sand between coats with 220-grit sandpaper. Allow it to dry.

2 Apply at least three thin coats of red/orange paint, alternating the direction of brushing with each one and allowing each to dry overnight. Aim for an even coverage without many brushstrokes. If the paint is difficult to spread, thin it slightly with no more than 20 percent mineral spirits. The thinner the paint, the more coats you will need to apply. Allow the final coat to dry for at least 24 hours.

3 Wet the surface slightly by misting water over the surface with the spray bottle before beginning to sand. Keep the surface wet while sanding. Work in small circular patterns using the 400-wet/dry sandpaper to remove all brushstrokes and imperfections. Wipe the surface frequently. The red should look and feel mirror smooth. Some of the black will begin to shadow through. Take your time, and slowly reveal the beauty.

4 After determining the natural wear patterns, use the 600-wet/dry sandpaper to "pull out" the black. Use a back-and-forth sanding motion until the black begins to appear; then use a combination of circular and back-and-forth sanding patterns for the most natural look. Create irregular black areas with tapering tops and bottoms. The black will come through an already shadowed area easier, and more believably.

5 When you are satisfied with your result, clean the surface with a soft cloth, and allow it to dry. Topcoat with one or two coats of varnish.

2 | Steel Wool Stria

THIS VERSATILE TECHNIQUE gives you a soft, linear, textural pattern. It's appropriate for any piece of furniture, whether traditional or contemporary.

Although it stands on its own merit, try it as a background for painted embellishments or other finishes. Achieve an interesting look by stamping or painting a freehand design and then using the *Steel Wool Stria* technique over it.

Adjust the degree of transparency by mixing more or less paint to glazing liquid. Mix more glazing liquid into the paint for a more transparent glaze.

Here's a general rule of thumb for choosing your colors: if your basecoat is light, use a darker glaze; if it's dark, use a lighter glaze; and with a medium value basecoat, either way works.

Refer to pages 7, 8, 14, and 16 to 17 before beginning.

MATERIALS AND TOOLS

- flat latex paint, medium gray
- flat latex paint, white
- latex glazing liquid
- water

- flat latex paintbrush, 3" (7.6 cm)
- cheesecloth, 90-weight
- steel wool pad, #2 grade
- dull/flat varnish

1 Basecoat the project surface with the medium gray paint until opaque; allow the paint to dry after each coat.
Note: You may use any type of paint, but if the basecoat is an oil-based paint, you *must* use an oil-based glaze. You may apply an oil-based glaze over latex paint.

2 Mix a glaze using one-part white paint, one-part glazing liquid, and slightly less than one-part water. Apply the glaze to an area small enough to allow you to complete the next two steps easily. Do *not* allow the glaze to dry as you work.

3 Pull through the glaze lightly, using a small wad of cheesecloth, and taking care not to remove all the glaze.
Tip: If you remove too much glaze and your surface is still wet, brush on some more.

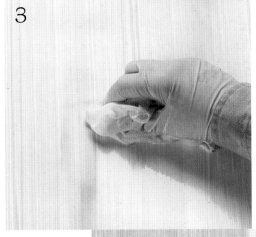

4 Drag the steel wool pad through the glaze using a medium steady pressure. Pull straight down or across the surface. You may do this more than once.

5 Topcoat with one or two coats of varnish.

3 | Mottled

SPRUCE UP just about anything using this mottled finish. Although mottling may be rendered with graphically hard edges, aim for soft and billowy. You want to see the three values of color—light, medium, and dark—without discerning where each color starts and stops.

With this easy finish, you apply paint straight from the can—no mixing glazes! Latex paint is most often used, but if you choose oil-based paint, a very softly blended look develops.

This finish is flexible and adaptable. To give this highly contemporary finish an antique feel, use deep browns. For a self-sealed surface, use paints with different sheens. It's even easy to touch up bangs and bumps if you record the paint colors used when you apply the finish.

The paint must stay wet while you work this finish. The finish develops in a sequence. You'll apply light, then medium, then dark paint, covering a smaller area, and then you'll repeat the sequence. Simply wipe, no need to clean, the brush between paint colors.

Refer to *French Brush* (page 19) and pages 7, 8, and 14 before beginning.

- latex primer, white
- 4" (10.2 cm) flat latex paintbrush
- flat latex paint, white
- flat latex paint, beige
- flat latex paint, gray

1 Basecoat the project surface with the primer.

2 Load the paintbrush generously with the white paint and apply, using the French brush technique over about 75 percent of the surface (if small) or not larger than a 12" × 12" (30.5 × 30.5 cm) area. Wipe the paintbrush on a rag or paper towel, but do not clean. Load the paintbrush generously with the beige paint and apply in and around the white paint, covering approximately 40 percent of the project surface.

3 Load the paintbrush with the gray paint (use less than the other colors), and apply in and around the beige and white areas, covering about 15 percent of the surface.
Tip: Imagine the gray as a shadow and the most buried color. It is the gray that allows the finish to have depth and it should move through the surface.

4 Apply more white and blend it into the gray; pick up the beige and blend; pick up the gray and blend. Continue this rhythm until the entire piece is painted.
Tip: Try to avoid blotches. Think of working back and forth among the colors and in and out of various areas.

5 Topcoat with one or two coats of varnish.

4 | Textured Plaster

SOMETIMES THE MOST common object creates an uncommon look. This very textural finish appears much more sophisticated than the material used to achieve it—an ordinary fiberglass window screen.

Although especially suitable for contemporary designs and flat surfaces, the *Textured Plaster* technique can be used on a traditional piece for an interesting visual contrast.

This piece was created using a random pattern to apply and to remove the plastering compound. You can achieve other looks by using an even application or removing in an all-over pattern. Make sure the piece of screen you use is slightly larger than the project surface for ease when handling. Screening comes in many widths, giving you the opportunity to work on almost any size project.

Refer to page 14 before beginning.

MATERIALS AND TOOLS

- all-purpose joint compound
- white glue, Elmer's® Glue-all
- spreading knife, 6" (15.2 cm)
- screen material, fiberglass
- sandpaper, 150-grit
- eggshell latex paint

- latex paintbrush, 4" (10.2 cm)
- flat oil-based paint, light beige
- mineral spirits
- flat oil paintbrush, 3" (7.6 cm)
- cheesecloth, 90-weight
- flat oil-based varnish

1 No basecoat is necessary with this technique. The wood may be unfinished, painted, or varnished. If varnished or painted, sand with 150-grit sandpaper to roughen.

2 Mix nine-parts all-purpose joint compound with *exactly* one-part white glue. Apply randomly to the surface leaving some voids and low spots.

3 Place a flat piece of fiberglass screen over the wet joint compound. Press the screen into the wet compound with the spreading blade; then remove the excess compound from the back of the screen. Remove the screen and allow the surface to dry completely.

4 Sand lightly to remove any burrs and nubs. Apply two coats of latex paint to the entire surface using the latex paintbrush. Avoid flooding the screen indentations with paint. Allow the paint to dry.

5 Thin the oil-based paint to skim milk consistency with mineral spirits, and apply using the oil paintbrush. Allow the paint to dry only until it takes on a matte look (usually 10 to 20 minutes). Do not allow it to dry completely. With a piece of cheesecloth slightly dampened with mineral spirits, remove the oil-based paint from the surface, leaving paint in the recessed areas.

6 Topcoat with one or two coats of varnish.

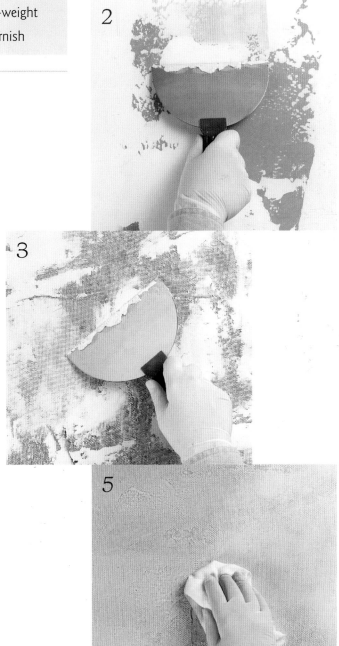

2

3

5

WONDERING WHAT TO DO with the many photographs stored in your computer? Take them beyond a scrapbook or a silver frame set on a table— let them become the table! Imagine a child's headboard covered with favorite images. This finish is not decoupage, but a modern application of paper to a piece of furniture. Whether following a theme or choosing random much-loved photos, your work is sure to be a conversation piece.

A computer, a basic photo-editing program, and a printer allow flexibility, as you can manipulate the size and color of the images, but photocopies can be used as long as they are produced on matte-finish photo-grade paper. Photocopying allows you to change color into black and white, and

5 | Photo Montage

alter the size of the image to fit the surface as well. Stiffer magazine covers also work, offering themes for teens to toddlers.

When working with photographic images, never use your originals. Store them in a safe place and use copies.

The images used in this project started as color photographs. After duplicating the image in an editing program, the copy was converted to a sepia tone to add a bit of age.

For best results, print your images on matte-finish photo-grade computer printing paper.

Refer to pages 7, 8, and 14 before beginning.

- flat latex paint, black
- matte finish photo-grade computer printing paper
- wallpaper cutting blade
- metal straightedge or ruler

- chalk, white
- blue painter's tape
- smooth, acid-free artist sketchbook pad, 18" × 24" (45.7 × 61 cm)

- spray adhesive, 3M Spray 77®
- wax paper
- rubber roller
- satin oil-based varnish

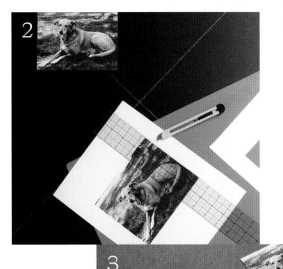

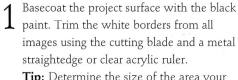

1 Basecoat the project surface with the black paint. Trim the white borders from all images using the cutting blade and a metal straightedge or clear acrylic ruler.
Tip: Determine the size of the area your photocopies will cover and which photos will be placed "portrait" or "landscape." Size your images appropriately before printing.

2 Draw two diagonal lines with chalk to find the center intersection of the surface. Locating the center helps facilitate a balanced composition.

3 Place a number of images on the surface and move them around until you find a pleasing composition. Keep your composition in place by sticking a loop of painter's tape *very lightly* to the back of one image, then replace it. Repeat with all the photos.

4 Lift one image and remove its tape. Lay the image back side up on a clean sketchbook page. Lightly apply an even coat of spray adhesive across the entire back. Place the image back carefully, for you will *not* be able to reposition it.

5 Place a sheet of wax paper over the image. Roll it smooth using the rubber roller and flatten any bubbles or air pockets. Smooth with clean fingers if necessary. Repeat steps 4 and 5 with all images. Allow the surface to dry for 24 hours.

6 Topcoat with one or two coats of satin oil-based varnish.
Tip: When applying the varnish, the photo paper may bubble. Don't worry. Press the image flat with a fingertip once the varnish is dry.

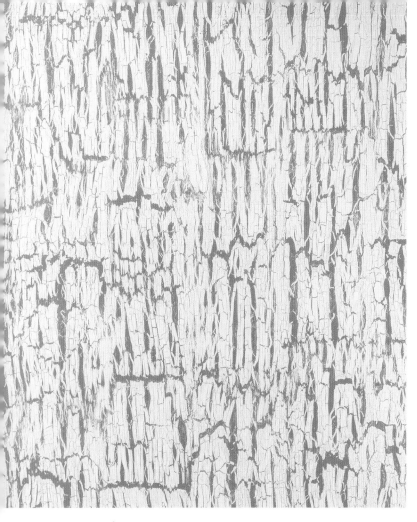

6 | Crackle

A CRACKLED FINISH is fun on just about anything. The weathered look rescues even battered furniture, giving it shabby chic style.

Crackles can be as large as in the example shown or as fine as the cracks in porcelain. You control the size of the crackle by the type of crackle product used and by varying the thickness of the overcoat paint.

There are many crackle products; however, the best choice is crackle from a paint store rather than a craft store. The containers are larger and the medium is less expensive. Check the label to find out if you are purchasing a large- or small-crackle material.

An overglaze of dark gel stain antiques the finish further. It's a lovely option, especially if you are using small porcelain crackle material.

Refer to pages 7, 8, 10, 11, and 14 before beginning.

- eggshell latex paint, gray
- flat latex paint, white
- flat latex paintbrush, 4" (10.2 cm)
- hair dryer (optional)
- gel stain (optional)
- crackle medium, Modern Masters® Crackle
- flat oil-based varnish

1 Basecoat the project surface with the gray paint.

2 Apply a thin, even coat of the crackle medium with the paintbrush. Allow it to dry for at least one hour.

3 Use full-bodied white paint (straight from the can) to achieve the cracks pictured here. Apply the paint with an even stroke from top to bottom.
Note: If you reload the paintbrush, continue painting where you left off. Avoid over-brushing. Do not brush back and forth.
Tip: Instead of using a paintbrush to apply the crackle medium and the paint, you may use a skinny foam roller. Roll in a straight one-way direction, slightly overlapping adjacent sections.

4 After you have applied the paint over the entire surface, you can force-dry the cracks with a hair dryer.

5 If desired, apply a coat of gel stain following the instructions under *All About Stains* (page 13) to further age your surface.

6 Topcoat with one or two coats of varnish. Apply *only* an oil-based varnish, as a water-based varnish will dissolve the crackle material.

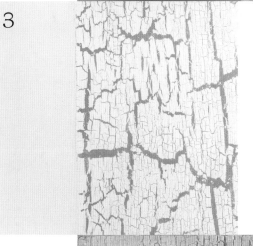

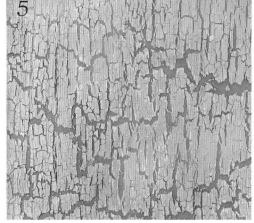

PUTTING TWO INCOMPATIBLE products together can cause a wonderful reaction. This stunning abstract finish was created with just one color over a basecoat.

If the richness of this deep blue intrigues you, use Japan Color paint. The Japan Color palette contains numerous, beautifully deep colors that match artist oil colors. They are sold in small 6-ounce (170 g) cans—no waste with quarts!

Most important, Japan Color dries flat. Standard paint-store paint only approaches this depth of color with paints that have a sheen (such as eggshell), and this technique requires a flat paint.

7 | Broken Paint

The blue used on this surface is Japan Color ultramarine blue. The basecoat is a very light gray. The gray basecoat offers a subtle contrast. To reduce the contrast even further, use a darker gray basecoat. For a higher contrast, use a white basecoat.

Refer to pages 7, 8, and 14 before beginning.

MATERIALS AND TOOLS

- eggshell latex paint, light gray
- foam roller, 4" (10.2 cm)
- mineral spirits
- Japan Color, ultramarine blue
- two paint pails

- flat oil paintbrush, 3" (7.6 cm)
- hair dryer
- oval sash paintbrush, 2" (5.1 cm)
- T-shirt rags
- oil-based varnish

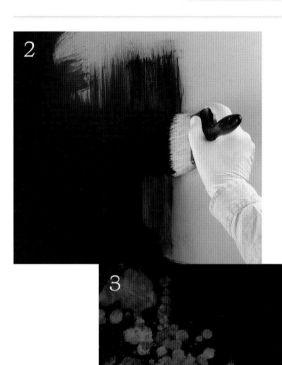

1 Basecoat the project surface with the light gray paint using the foam roller. Allow to dry overnight to cure (harden) the paint so the surface isn't absorbent.

2 Thin the ultramarine blue to a whole milk consistency with mineral spirits in a paint pail. Apply one coat using the flat paintbrush.

3 Dry the just applied blue paint with a hair dryer only until the shine disappears (the paint must be fresh to "bloom" properly. Do not over dry. Pour a small amount of mineral spirits into a pail. Dip the oval sash paintbrush about 1" (2.5 cm) into the mineral spirits. Hold the paintbrush close to, but not touching, the painted surface, letting the mineral spirits drip onto it. Continue the dipping and dripping until you've covered a small area, then blot the drips with a T-shirt rag. You may need to apply a little pressure or rub the surface slightly to remove the blue paint. Keep turning your rag to a clean spot to avoid depositing paint back onto the surface.

4 Continue step 3 until you are happy with the results. You can vary the depth by how much ultramarine blue you remove with the rag. If too much mineral spirits fall on the surface, or if you don't like the pattern of drips, don't touch the surface. Simply allow the mineral spirits to dry and then you may repeat the dripping process.
Tip: If the contrast is too high, overglaze (page 12) after 24 hours using the ultramarine blue paint.

5 Topcoat with one or two coats of varnish.

8 Intarsia

THE WORD *INTARSIA* comes from the Latin *interserere*, which means "to insert." Historically, intarsia meant an inlaid wood pattern. It is believed the technique developed in Italy in or around the 14th and 15th centuries.

Marble intarsia can be seen on the floors of buildings and churches throughout Europe. Marble and stone were inlaid in fanciful patterns or pictorial motifs such as lion heads and astrological symbols.

Intarsia creates pattern, color, form,

and shape and is a wonderful way to include the look of semi-precious stone without the high cost or specialized knowledge necessary. With a combination of painting techniques, you can create a simple or highly involved design.

Malachite, lapis, and stone, each outlined in *Fabulous Fakes*, were used in this intarsia, but you can use any finish you like. Refer to the specific instructions to apply the finishes, and to pages 7, 8, and 14 before beginning.

MATERIALS AND TOOLS

- clear ruler, 24" (61 cm)
- pencil
- blue painter's tape, 1" (2.5 cm)
- flat latex paint, white
- latex paintbrush, 4" (10.2 cm)
- eggshell latex paint, pale yellow/green
- painter's paper, 3" (7.6 cm)
- latex paint, gold
- satin oil-based varnish
- All other materials and tools listed under *Malachite* (page 78), *Provincial Lapis* (page 98), and *Faux Stone*, (page 80).

1 Basecoat the project surface with the white paint using the paintbrush. Allow the paint to dry. Mark off the intarsia design area with the ruler and pencil, then tape along the outside of the design area on which you are working.

2 Draw your pattern with a thin pencil line using a clear ruler (which helps keep lines parallel or perpendicular to each other).

3 Tape along the outside of the pencil lines beginning in the interior of the design. Basecoat each section with the appropriate paint for the individual finishes, allowing the paint to dry between sections. In this case, the pale yellow/green paint was applied for the Malachite finish. Sand lightly after all the sections have dried. Follow the instructions under *Malachite* (page 78) to complete the center section. Allow to dry overnight; then remove the tape.

4 Tape the small squares along the outside of the pencil lines, inserting painter's paper along the outside edges. Basecoat the small squares with the gold paint. Allow to dry, and sand lightly. Follow the instructions under *Provincial Lapis* (page 98) to complete the squares. Allow to dry overnight, and then remove the tape.

5 Tape the rectangular sections outside of the white, securing the tape well by burnishing pressing (rubbing firmly) with your fingertips. Follow the instructions under *Faux Stone* (page 80) to complete the squares. Allow to dry, and then remove the tape.

6 Topcoat with one or two coats of varnish.

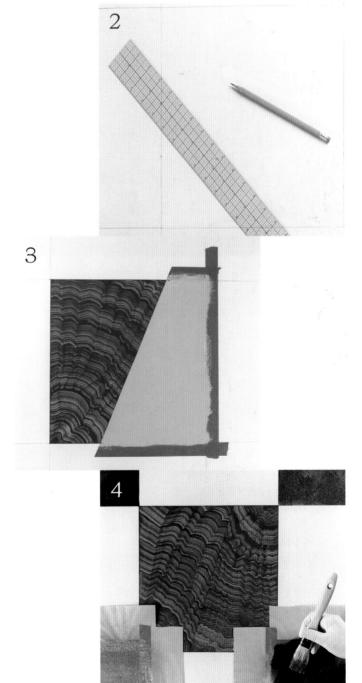

9 | Striping

PAINTING A STRIPE onto a piece of furniture may seem intimidating, but you'll quickly become good at it with a bit of practice.

Your stripe need not be perfect—remember, you're not a machine. Slight inconsistencies and unevenness merely reveal a bit of hand-painted personality.

It helps to have a good striping paintbrush. A striping paintbrush has long, soft, and flexible hairs that hold a good quantity of paint. Art materials stores sell high-quality striping brushes. The paintbrush size determines the width of the stripe, so consider purchasing both a #6 and a #3 sable striping paintbrush.

Location determines what style of stripe you will create. Thin accent stripes are done in indentations, wider bands on turned surfaces, and a variety of widths can be done along the edges of a surface.

Relax, practice, and look where you want the stripe to go—your hand will follow—and you will be making a steady and beautiful stripe in no time.

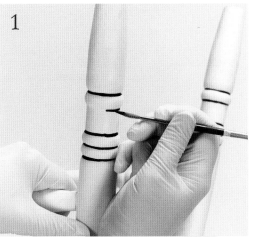

1 To create an incised stripe, thin the paint slightly with water or mineral spirits, as appropriate. Load the sable striping paintbrush with the thinned paint. Place the paintbrush tip into an indentation, and pull it toward yourself.

2 To create a broad, or band stripe, pick up slightly thinned paint on the ¼" (6 mm) paintbrush, hold it at a 45 degree angle to the surface, and pull it toward yourself.

3 Make a guide when you are striping a flat surface with no indentations. The guide can help create an even width for band striping or a line for a thin stripe. The guide is constructed the same way for both.

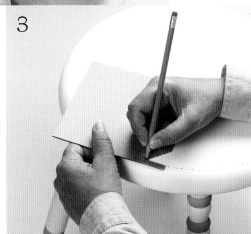

Determine the width of the band or the proximity of the stripe to the edge of your furniture piece. Mark the top edge of a square of cardboard that distance from the left side. Add a second mark 1" (2.5 cm) straight down from the first mark. Place another mark along the top edge of the cardboard 1" (2.5 cm) from the first mark. Draw a line from the first mark to the second, and from the second to the last mark. Create a notch by cutting along the lines with a craft knife.

Hold the guide with its left side resting along the edge of the project surface. Hold a pencil in your other hand, and place its point at the inside of the notch. Gently draw both the guide and the pencil long the edge to create a guideline. Load the paintbrush well with thinned paint and either draw it toward yourself along the pencil line (striping paintbrush) or between the edge and the pencil line (flat paintbrush).

10 | Soft Geometry

LOOK WHAT HAPPENS with a can of spray paint—a finish that creates itself!

Any color palette works, but using three colors to create *Soft Geometry* is easiest. The three colors should include a light, a medium, and a dark value.

Relax and enjoy the process as you create this soft look. If you think too much, your work will look labored. You will know how much to do and when to stop—when you like it!

Make sure you use a drop cloth and paint only in a well-ventilated area or outside if the day is not windy.

Refer to pages 7, 8, and 14 before beginning.

1 Basecoat the project surface with the medium-dark gray paint.

2 Create the blue corners by resting the cardboard shield on the project surface at a 45 degree angle. The edges of the shield need to extend beyond the edges of the furniture piece. Point the spray can away from the shield, with the spray nozzle pointed toward the furniture piece. Mist the paint over the surface moving your arm and lightly covering the surface with paint. Do three corners of varying sizes in medium blue, allowing the paint to dry between corners.

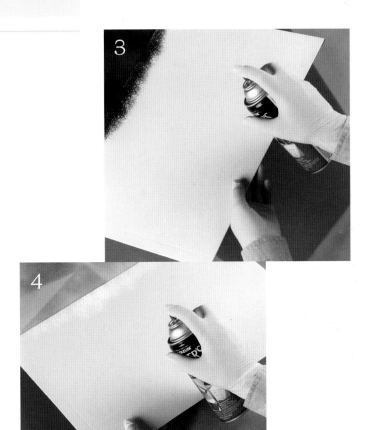

3 Mist black (or the darkest color) over the fourth corner.
Note: Aim for see-through coverage; avoid opaque buildup. The darkest color will be applied very lightly.

4 Position the shield; spray with white (or the lightest color). Repeat as many times, in different areas, as you like, allowing the paint to dry between areas. Some sections will become denser as the paint coats overlap creating a "soft" geometry.

5 Position the shield; mist using the medium blue (or your mid-tone color) paint. This step adds depth and interest.

6 Spray the final layer areas with white (or your lightest color).

7 Topcoat with one or two coats of varnish.

11 | Torn Paper

THE *TORN PAPER* finish is amazingly simple, quick, and effective. It's best suited for modern or contemporary furniture, as it softens straight lines by adding a subtle tactile and visual texture.

There are two important concepts to keep in mind when using this finish. One: Have enough paper. Two: Keep the paper and the application area clean.

Using an artist sketchbook drawing pad allows you to flip to a clean, flat sheet each time you need to tear and glue. Too many sheets of floppy, loose paper can lead to frustration with glue and paper sticking to everything—you, the dog, the cat—you get the idea.

Choose smooth-surfaced furniture pieces with closed grain (open grain can cause air-pocket problems). The glued paper may be applied directly over any surface that does not resist water. If your surface is water-resistant, apply a primer coat before beginning.

MATERIALS AND TOOLS

- white glue, Elmer's® Glue-all
- water
- flat latex paintbrush, 4" (10.2 cm)

- smooth artist acid-free sketch-book pad, 18" (45.7 cm) × 24" (61 cm), paper weight 50 lb
- rubber roller, 4" (10.2 cm) to 6" (15.2 cm)

- wallpaper cutting blade
- satin oil-based paint, off-white
- oil paintbrush, 4"(10.2 cm)

1 Thin the white glue with water to brushing consistency; apply it to the project surface using the latex paintbrush (this helps the paper adhere strongly to the surface). Allow it to dry completely, about one hour. The glue is completely transparent when dry.

2 Tear one or two edges of a sheet of paper into soft, irregularly curved lines (avoid straight lines). Brush glue over the entire back of the paper, covering it completely. Avoid getting glue on the face of the paper. **Tip:** Add a few drops of food coloring to the glue to help you see it better against the white paper.

3 Lay the paper smoothly, glue-side down, on the project surface, extending it slightly beyond the surface. Firmly secure the paper and roll out any air pockets with the rubber roller.
Tip: Use your fingertips to gently press out any small air bubbles. Don't worry about an occasional wrinkle, as it will lend itself to the look, but keep wrinkles to a minimum.

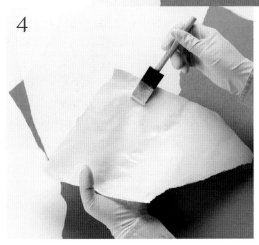

4 Continue tearing, gluing, and laying various shapes of paper, overlapping the other pieces as you work. Voids become part of the look when painted. To wrap edges, fold the paper over them and cut the paper at the corners to form a clean edge. Do not fold excess paper around the corners.

5 When the paper is completely dry, trim off any excess with the wallpaper knife. Apply the off-white paint using the oil paintbrush. **Note:** If you prefer to use latex paint, you must seal the papered surface completely with shellac prior to applying the paint. There is no need to topcoat, as the satin oil-based paint is very durable.

MAKE A STATEMENT—the unexpected is a delightful twist on an otherwise uninteresting surface. Have a bit of fun with words applied to furniture by using affirmations, names, a favorite saying, or your own poetic words.

12 | Words and Numbers

Stencil the kitchen chairs with family nicknames, ring the dining table with "bon appétit," or liven up the picnic table with the message "Ants Beware." Keep your pile of recipes clipped from newspapers and magazines right at hand, but cleverly hidden in a painted box stenciled with "Yum."

A stencil is the easiest way to apply lettering to furniture, but the stenciled effect may be eliminated by painting connections between the letters with an artist's paintbrush after the stenciled paint has dried.

- pencil
- blue painter's tape, 1" (2.5 cm)
- ruler or tape measure
- paper
- alphabet stencil, 1" (2.5 cm)
- stencil brush, ½" (1.3 cm)
- satin oil-based paint
- paper towels
- angled artist brush, ⅛" (optional)

1 Determine (and mark, if necessary) the length of the path on which to stencil the letters. Place blue painter's tape along the bottom of the path. Find the middle of the path and mark the midpoint on the painter's tape.
Tip: Place a perpendicular piece of tape at the midpoint as a large visual aid.

2 Write out your saying in block letters on a piece of paper. Count the number of spaces between, and number of letters in, each word. Divide the total by two. To find the center, count, starting at the first letter, to that number. You will position the first half of your saying to left of the center mark.

Apply the letters from the center moving left (which means "writing" backward, so use care not to misspell). Keep your written saying in front of you and cross off the letters as you work. Continue until the first half is completed.
Tip: Use the spacing between the letters on the stencil to keep letters equal distances apart. Use the letter X to define the space between words. Stencils are usually clear or somewhat transparent, so you will be able to easily place the bottom of the letter along the tape line.

3 Tape the stencil in place, dip the stencil brush in the paint, and tap off the excess on a paper towel. Using a pouncing motion, stencil the first letter. Remove the stencil and clean off the paint around the letter. Allow the paint to dry or force-dry with a hair dryer, then proceed with the next letter to the left.
Tip: Using oil-based paint allows you to easily remove a misaligned or incorrect letter with mineral spirits.

4 Move back to the center and stencil the letters toward the right until all of your words have been stenciled.

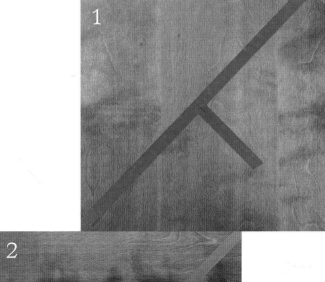

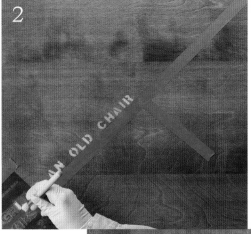

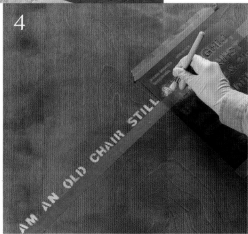

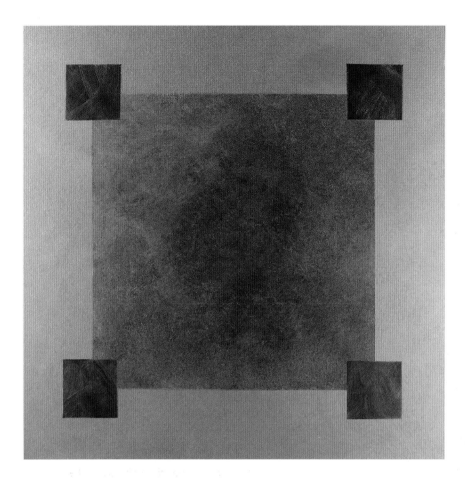

13 | From the Can

APPLY THIS METALLIC finish straight from the container. No mixing or adjustments needed!

Suitable for enhancing an entire large tabletop or as a decorative inset, the *From the Can* finish also adds a lovely accent to a wooden box lid. This versatile finish says contemporary, yet the formal colors allow it to speak in a traditional voice as well.

The design here is geometric, but organic or abstract shapes offer a striking modern statement. Snip into the "away" edge of the painter's tape to mark off curves.

When using painter's tape, be sure to remove it while the paint is still wet as the tape may pull dried paint away.

Refer to *French Brush* (page 19), and pages 7, 8, and 14 before beginning.

- flat latex primer
- flat latex paintbrush, 3" (7.6 cm)
- Modern Masters® Champagne, ME 206 opaque

- pencil
- ruler
- blue painter's tape, 1" (2.5 cm)
- painter's taping paper

- Modern Masters® Sapphire, ME 655 semi-opaque
- oval sash brush, 2" (5.1 cm)
- cheesecloth, 90-weight
- flat latex paintbrush, 1" (2.5 cm)

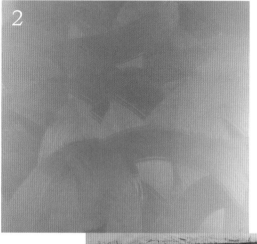

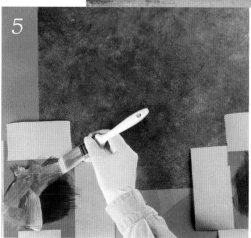

1 Basecoat the project surface with primer using the latex brush. Allow to dry one hour. Repeat with a second coat.

2 Apply a coat of champagne paint using the flat latex paintbrush and the French brush technique. Allow the paint to dry one hour. Repeat with a second coat.

3 Using a ruler and a pencil, mark off a 4" (10.2 cm) border. Apply the painter's tape along the outside of the pencil lines, securing painter's paper along the outside edges. Press and rub the tape with your fingers to avoid gaps.

Apply a coat of sapphire paint using the French brush technique. Remove the tape; allow the paint to dry, or force-dry with a hair dryer. Repeat with a second coat

4 Pounce (page 19) the champagne paint over the surface working quickly with a slightly water-dampened cheesecloth, to soften the paint. Remove the tape and the paper. Allow the paint to dry about 30 minutes.

5 Mark off a small square that slightly overlaps one corner of the interior square. Apply painter's tape and paper along the marks. Paint the small square with two coats of the sapphire paint. Remove the tape. Allow the paint to dry. Repeat for each corner.

Apply one thin coat of champagne over the sapphire, either brushing the color on using curved brush strokes with the sash brush or pouncing it on with cheesecloth to create texture. Allow the paint to dry; then remove the tape and paper.

6 Topcoat with one or two coats of varnish.

STAMPING IS a wonderfully easy way to apply decorative motifs to a surface. The selection of rubber stamps is wide and varied; you will find unlimited motifs, themes, and designs. Go to any craft store and you will find a stamp or two that you will want to incorporate into a furniture piece, guaranteed!

If you plan to stamp with ink, ask your salesperson if the ink you've selected can be covered by a varnish. Most can, but checking is always best. Apply a varnish coat over the stamped surface to protect the ink.

14 | Stamping

To stamp small areas, add stamping medium to acrylic paint. You'll find both of those products in craft stores.

Whether you plan to stamp a border or a center motif, practice loading the proper amount of ink on the stamp and placing the stamp to properly line up the design. If the stamp's design is smaller than its wooden back, make yourself a guide: stamp the design on paper, cut it out, and tape or paste it to the top of the stamp. Aligning will be much easier.

- ruler or tape measure
- pencil
- stamp
- inkpad
- paper (optional)

1 To create a perfect square or rectangular border, measure the length and width of the stamp design, then use multiples of the length plus one width-measurement to determine the length of a stamped line. Draw lines the appropriate length forming a square or rectangle on the project surface. Place the inked stamp at one corner, press lightly on the stamp, but do not rock it. Lift, re-ink, and continue stamping along the line. When you reach the end of the first line, a space the width of the stamp will remain. Place the stamp parallel to the second pencil line, and continue stamping. Repeat the procedure at each corner.

2 If the border you want to stamp isn't evenly divisible by length of the stamp, use this "no precision" option.

Draw all the guidelines. Begin stamping along a line, placing the inked stamp at one corner. Lift, re-ink, and continue stamping along the line. When you approach the end, tape a piece of paper along the adjacent line. Ink, then place the stamp, letting the overlap fall on the paper. Move the paper to the end of the next line, and continue stamping.

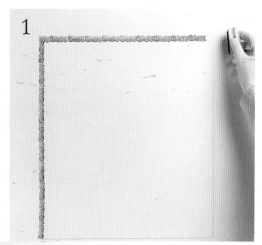

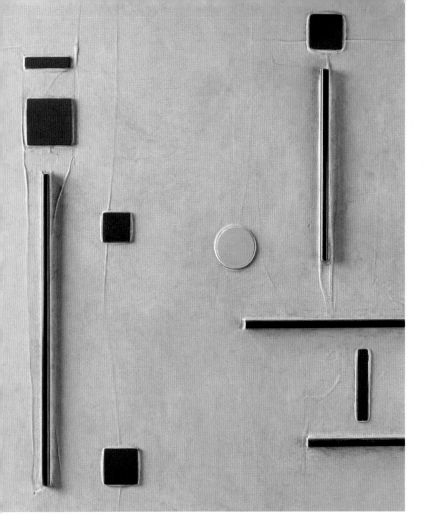

15   Found Objects

WITH *FOUND OBJECTS*, anything goes, from elegance to whimsy. Explore, find treasures, and then have fun with this technique. The little geometric plastic pieces shown here came from a salvage store.

Make this finish sophisticated by inserting brass strips or other elegant objects. Go monochromatic for a modern appeal by painting over the objects. Keep in mind that lightweight objects work better. This finish creates interest on boring cabinet sides or intrigue on a tabletop.

Flat objects work best, but experiment. If you use high-dimension objects, incorporate glass bumpers into your design and then set a piece of tempered glass on top of the surface. Your glass supplier can help you choose the appropriate glass top.

To begin, arrange your found objects in a pleasing design. Draw a diagram or take digital photographs to serve as a guide as you refine your arrangement. You will not be able to re-create a drawn design exactly, so just let it happen.

- found objects
- white glue, Elmer's® Glue-all
- Crazy Glue® or a two-part epoxy product (optional)
- measuring container, four-cup

- all-purpose joint compound
- flexible spreading blades, varied widths
- paintable latex caulk (optional)
- eggshell latex paint, white

- flat latex paint, gray
- latex glazing liquid
- flat latex paintbrush, 4" (10.2 cm)
- cheesecloth, 90-weight

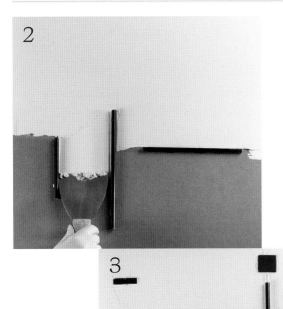

1 Glue objects no thicker than ¼" (6 mm) on the project surface with white glue. For objects that may not adhere with white glue, use Crazy Glue® or a two-part epoxy product.

2 Use the container to measure *exactly* one-part white glue to nine-parts joint compound (the glue adds durability). Mix well. Apply the compound smoothly (it's hard to sand), to a depth of ⅜" (9 cm) or less, over the entire surfce. Trowel marks may also be part of the design.
Tip: Place your objects farther apart than your smallest size spreading blade.

3 While the joint compound is still wet, place the smaller objects into it using a slight twisting motion. Allow the compound to ooze up around the object to hold it in place. Allow the compound to dry completely. Lightly sand out any nibs or roughness.
Tip: Once the compound is dry, you may run a bead of caulk around the larger objects to ensure adhesion.

4 Basecoat the project surface with two coats of white paint; allow the paint to dry. Mix a glaze using one-part gray paint and one-part glazing liquid to one-part water. Apply the glaze using the 4" (10.2 cm) paintbrush. Immediately pounce with a wad of cheesecloth to soften.
Tip: Apply the glaze over the objects; then use a water-dampened cloth to wipe off the glaze before it dries. If the glaze dries and cannot be removed with water, try using denatured alcohol. It removes the glaze from most objects.

5 Topcoat with one or two coats of varnish.

THIS FUN PAINT turns any surface into a magnet. It's great for kids' rooms, even though it only comes in a dark charcoal gray color—simply paint over it using any finish technique you like. The *Mottled* finish (page 23) was used on the project shown. The magnets will still stick. Of course, if you are using a light colored paint, you may want to apply a primer over the magnetic paint.

Paint a small rectangle on a storage drawer and label it with magnetic letters. Amuse your child by painting his or her door and attaching magnetic

16 | Magnetic Paint

photo frames, objects, letters, or poetry. Paint a wall; then glue small magnets to each corner of school artwork, and create a gallery of "floating" art.

No more need to tape notes and whatnot to your door or wall! Hold notes with a decorative magnet. The magnetic charge is too weak to hold heavy objects, but strong enough to hold pictures, newspaper or magazine clippings, and photos.

You'll find magnetic paint in paint and home improvement stores.

Refer to *French Brush* (page 19), *Mottled* (page 28), and pages 7 and 8 before beginning.

- magnetic paint
- angled latex paintbrush, 2" (5.1 cm)
- sandpaper, 220-grit
- All other materials and tools listed under *Mottled* (page 28).

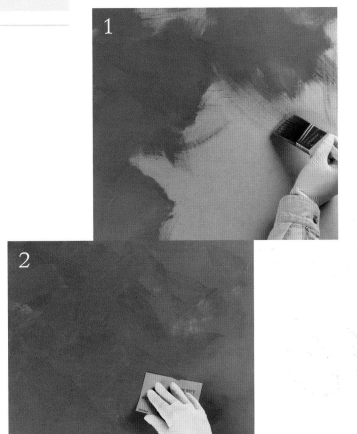

1 Apply the first coat of magnetic paint to a prepared project surface, using the French brush technique. Do not overwork the paint. Allow the paint to dry according to the paint manufacturer's instructions.

2 Apply the second coat using the same procedure as in step 1. The heavier the coating of magnetic paint applied, the stronger the magnetic attraction becomes. When dry, sand with 220-grit sandpaper.

Tip: This paint is very thick and grainy, so consider using an appealing texture over it. Follow the directions under *Mottled* (page 28), or use any preferred technique to cover the magnetic paint. Apply the magnetic paint with the same brushing technique as the chosen finish so the brushstrokes mimic each other.

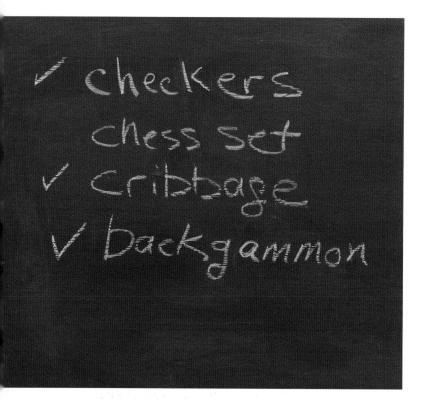

CHALKBOARD PAINT just lends itself to fun. Paint a square on a commonly used furniture piece and leave messages for family members. Paint on children's tables or other furniture pieces to inspire them to have fun decorating their own furniture while you apply one of the *50 Ways to Paint Furniture* finishes to a piece of yours. Paint the inside of an armoire and their artwork can be hidden away.

17 Chalkboard Paint

Chalkboard paint is a smooth, almost flat, black paint that goes on beautifully with either a paintbrush or a roller.

Black and green are most commonly found, but a wide range of bright, cheery colors can be ordered from most paint stores or online.

Refer to *Basecoats* (page 16 and 17) before beginning.

- chalkboard paint
- angle-edged latex paintbrush,
  3" (7.6 cm)

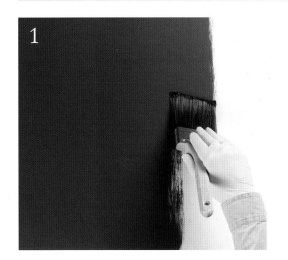

1 Apply the chalkboard paint over a properly primed surface. Hold the paintbrush at a 45 degree angle, and apply at least three coats, allowing the paint to dry between coats. Follow the manufacturer's instructions for drying times. The paint should cure 24 hours (harden) before using chalk on the surface.

If you apply painter's tape to an area, remove the tape immediately after painting (while the paint is still wet), as the dried paint on the tape may lift or chip the paint on the surface.

Tip: Chalkboard paint has a good shelf life, so store it in a heated environment and use it periodically to refresh your painted piece.

18 | Checkerboard Tabletop

A CHECKERBOARD PAINTED right on the tabletop is a wonderful addition to a children's room but also makes an adult game table attractive and doubly useful. The pattern used is the regulation layout for either chess or checkers.

While the instructions tell how to paint the checkerboard over a raw wood surface, you may also create it on a painted surface (and in any colors if the authenticity of the regulation board isn't a consideration).

The squares may be any size. You can easily alter the size of the checker-

board by dividing one of the edges by eight. Mark each edge using that measurement.

The number of squares must remain constant in order to use the board. The regulation chess/checkerboard consists of a field of 8 squares across and 8 squares down, totaling 64 squares. As a player faces the board, the square in the lower left-hand side is black and the lower right-hand square is red. This is the proper orientation, so lay out your board accordingly.

Refer to page 14 before beginning.

MATERIALS AND TOOLS

- ruler
- pencil
- blue painter's tape, 2" (5.1 cm)
- flat latex paint, red
- wallpaper cutting blade
- flat latex paint, black
- sponge paintbrushes, 1" (2.5 cm)
- wet/dry sandpaper, 400-grit
- white eraser
- tack cloth
- soft rag
- gel stain, Old Masters®, Golden Oak

1 Draw a 16" (40.6 cm) square in the center of your tabletop. Apply painter's tape along the outline. Paint the interior with one coat of red paint. Allow the paint to dry.

2 Mark the perimeter every 2" (5.1 cm). Draw a pencil line from every mark to the one directly opposite.

3 Run the tape along the inside of the left pencil line from top to bottom. Mark off the eight squares. Beginning with the *lower left square*, initial all the squares to be *cut out* with a "B." Cut out and remove them using the wallpaper blade and a ruler.

   Run another piece of tape along the edge of the row of squares and repeat the procedure, alternating the "B" squares. Continue until the checkerboard is complete. Press the edges of the tape firmly with your fingers.

4 Apply one coat of black paint using the 1" (2.5 cm) paintbrush.
Tip: Brush the black paint from the tape into the square to help avoid bleeding.

5 When the paint sheen dulls (about one hour), it is dry. Remove the tape.

6 Very lightly sand in the direction of the wood grain. If a bit of paint lifts, it will create a "worn" look, which is fine. Tack (wipe) to remove the sanding grit. Erase any pencil marks.

7 With a clean, soft rag, apply the gel stain to the entire surface and immediately wipe off to soften. Allow the stain to dry for 24 hours. Lightly sand again, as the staining might have raised the grain. Tack the surface.

8 Topcoat with one or two coats of varnish.

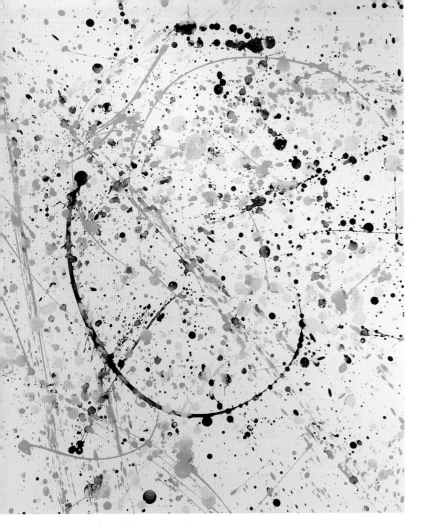

RELEASE YOUR JACKSON Pollock urges. Invite your children to assist. This whimsical and active finish looks spectacular done in the right colors on the right surface. It's perfect for the "retro" look, and fun on something unexpected.

The most difficult element to this finish is stopping—but do so when it makes you smile!

Experiment with a dark basecoat and light "drip and spill" paints. Amuse the children by using a "glow-in-the-dark" paint as one of the colors on a table for them.

19 | Drip and Spill

Even though this finish looks a bit chaotic, you can achieve a graceful and sophisticated movement of paint and color on a surface. This is a bold and confident finish because there is no turning back—you will not be able to wipe off a mistake.

You'll feel like a conductor while creating this finish as you paint "from the shoulder" using your whole arm to move and flick the paintbrush.

Refer to pages 7, 8, and 14 before beginning.

- eggshell latex paint, white
- foam roller, 4" (10.2 cm)
- eggshell latex paint, off-white
- eggshell latex paint, tan
- eggshell latex paint, black

- water
- three paint pails
- three angle-edge latex brushes, 3" (7.6 cm)
- drop cloth, large

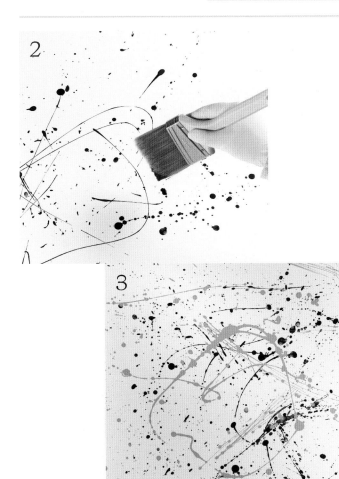

1 Basecoat the project surface with the white paint using the foam roller. Mix each of the other colors with water to a heavy cream consistency. Use a separate pail (and paintbrush) for each color.

2 Dip a paintbrush into the black paint. Hold it, point toward the project, about 3 ft (91.4 cm) above the surface. Let the paint drip as you move the paintbrush around, or create splatters by using your arm to flick the paintbrush in a sideways movement (flicking from the wrist constrains the pattern).

Create fine lines by holding the paintbrush close to the surface and letting the paint drip off the tip for at least 2 ft (61 cm) in a continuous string as you move the paintbrush. If the paint doesn't flow smoothly from the paintbrush, thin it with a bit more water, but do not thin it too much.

3 Vary the amount of each color used for a pleasing and harmonious composition. An equal amount of all three colors creates a dull look. Apply the tan paint using the procedures in step 2, but use 50 to 60 percent less "coverage" than that of the black paint.

4 Apply the off-white paint in the same manner, using 50 to 60 percent less "coverage" than that of the tan paint. Allow the surface to dry for two or three days.
Tip: If your proportions of any paint seem off, simply add more of the other colors until you have a pleasing balance. Just be careful that the paints don't get blended together.

5 Topcoat with one or two coats of varnish.

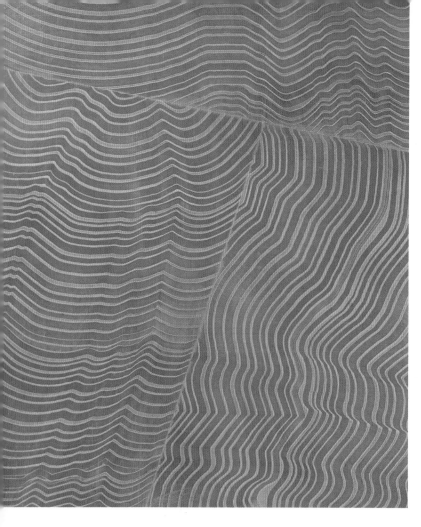

SQUEEGEE COMBING is an interesting, fun, and versatile finish that adds movement and interest to large flat surfaces.

Generally this finish is perceived as contemporary and modern. Render it with subtle tonal colorations such as ivory over white for an understated expression. Or use different paint sheen combinations; a red gloss over red flat for a sophisticated look. For high drama, try a high-contrast color scheme; white with black or deep burgundy.

20 | Squeegee Combing

Although a latex paint was used on this furniture piece, you may apply this finish with latex or oil-based paint. If you use oil-based paint, you will be able to "erase" by merely wiping out an area with mineral spirits. If you are confident and calm, use latex paint. Don't, however, use latex paint *over* oil-based paint, as the paint will lift.

Refer to *Basecoats* (page 16 and 17), and page14 before beginning.

- rubber squeegee, 6" (15.2 cm)
- craft knife
- eggshell latex paint, medium greenish-gray
- blue painter's tape, 1" (2.5 cm)

- angled-edge latex paintbrush, 3" (7.6 cm)
- eggshell latex paint, beige
- gel stain, Old Masters®, Dark Walnut
- rags

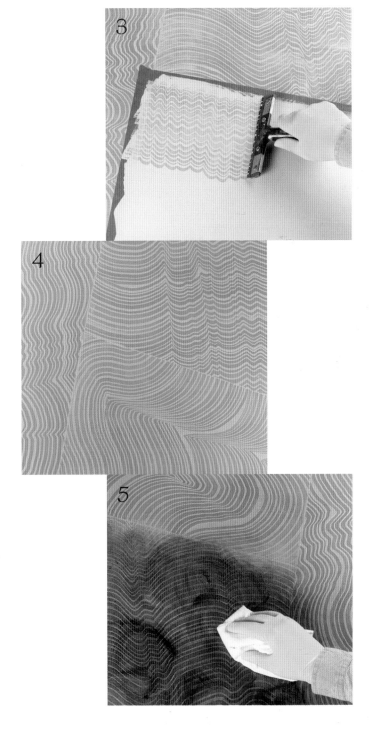

1 Cut inverted V-shaped notches along the edge of the squeegee with the craft knife. Vary the width of the notched areas and the distance between notches.

2 Basecoat the project surface with the greenish-gray paint. Allow the paint to dry.
Tip: A smooth basecoat helps the squeegee slide easily, yet if you have surface irregularities, they may lead to desirable "inconsistencies."

3 Divide your surface into sections, avoiding right angles (try for obtuse angles). Tape off one section. Brush slightly thinned beige paint over the section. Pull the notched squeegee through the wet paint, softly arcing and waving as you go. The type of pattern is up to you, soft or wild. Continue to follow your pattern over the entire section. You may add voids to your pattern by moving the squeegee farther over or slightly changing the angle of the pull. If you don't like how a section looks, wipe off the paint with a water-dampened cloth and start over. Allow the section to dry or force-dry with a hair dryer.
Tip: Thin the paint so it is only slightly "wetter." It should not run, but be loose enough to pull off with the squeegee.

4 Continue until all sections are completed, wiping the squeegee blade occasionally with a rag or paper towel to remove excess paint.

5 When all the sections are dry, apply the gel stain to soften and antique the finish. This will lower the contrast. Apply the gel stain with a rag and wipe off with a second rag until you create the desired look.

6 Topcoat with one or two coats of varnish.

Fabulous
FAKES

21 | Faux Tiles

SPRUCE UP YOUR tired old kitchen table or add interest to outdoor furniture.

Furniture pieces painted with the *Faux Tiles* finish will be seen up close, so the technique must look refined. The quickest and most successful way to achieve this is by creating a narrow grout line. Since ⅛" (3 mm) masking tape is difficult to find, you will need to spend a little extra time cutting your tape to the appropriate size—but the effort is well worth it.

Many of the finishes in *50 Ways to Paint Furniture* may be used to create the tile, particularly the *Faux Stone*, the *Marble*, the *Provincial Lapis*, and the *Malachite*.

Refer to *French Brush* (page 19), *Parchment* (page 68), and pages 7, 8, and 14 before beginning.

- flat latex paint, white
- flat latex paintbrush, 3" (7.6 cm)
- ruler or tape measure
- pencil
- blue painter's tape, 1" (2.5 cm)

- eraser
- wallpaper cutting blade
- flat latex paint, medium brown
- flat latex paint, medium-dark brown

- foam roller brush, 4" (10.2 cm)
- latex glazing liquid
- cheesecloth, 90-weight

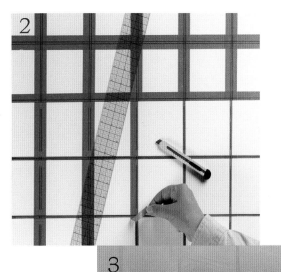

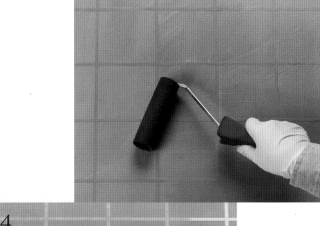

1 Basecoat the project surface with the white paint; allow the paint to dry overnight. Create a grid by dividing the length and width of the area to be "tiled" by the size of the tiles. For example, a tiled area 12" × 21" (30.5 × 53.3 cm) with 3" (7.6 cm) tiles creates a grid of four tiles down (12 divided by 3) and seven tiles across (21 divided by 3).

2 Pencil in all the grid lines on the project surface. Center the 1" (2.5 cm) painter's tape over each grid line. Create a ⅛" (3 mm) grout line by marking the center of the tape on both ends, then marking 1⁄16" (1.6 mm) to both sides of the center. Erase the center mark. Connect the marks on the opposite ends. Repeat on every tape line. Cut along all grout lines with the wallpaper blade, avoiding the areas where the grid lines cross, and remove the excess tape.

3 Work in a small area. Use the paintbrush to apply both brown paints using the French brush technique. Immediately soften the brushstrokes and blend the paint with the paint roller. Allow the paint to dry; remove the tape. Remove the penciled grid lines, if necessary.

4 Mix a glaze using one-part medium brown, one-part glazing liquid, and one-part water. Apply to the surface using the *Parchment* technique (page 68). While the glaze is wet, texture by pouncing the surface with a wad of cheesecloth. Allow the paint to dry completely.

5 Topcoat with one or two coats of varnish. If your project is to be used outdoors, use an exterior varnish.

THE *PARCHMENT* FINISH is one of the most foundational. This versatile finish radiates beauty on its own and as a base for stamped, stenciled, or painted decorative motifs. It can be used as an overglaze to age, reduce contrast, or lend depth to other finishes. Master this finish and have a myriad of possibilities open to you.

Whether you use oil-based or latex paint, the techniques used to create the finish are the same.

22 | Parchment

The *Parchment* finish should be soft, fairly even, and unobtrusive. Knowing when to stop manipulating the paint is key, as this finish will "get away" from you if you overwork it. Trust yourself, your hands, and your eyes, and a perfect result will quickly and effortlessly transpire. A subdued palette of earth-tones was used on the desk and shades of gray on the wood panel shown above, but the whole color spectrum is open to you.

Refer to pages 7, 8, and 14 before beginning.

MATERIALS AND TOOLS

- flat latex paint, white
- flat latex paint, brownish-gray
- latex glazing liquid
- water
- flat latex paintbrush, 4" (10.2 cm)
- cheesecloth, 90-weight, 36" (91.4 cm)

1 Basecoat the project surface with the white paint. You may want to basecoat a sample board to practice steps 3 and 4 before beginning to work on your project surface.

2 Mix a glaze using one-part brownish-gray paint, one-part glazing liquid, and one-part water. Apply the glaze, covering the surface completely, using the 4" (10.2 cm) paintbrush. This step does not have to be neat. Immediately move to step 3.

3 Slightly water-dampen the cheesecloth. Distribute the glaze to remove the brushstrokes, using a light pressure and a circular motion.

4 Soften the texture with a combination pat-and-wipe using a clean, water-dampened 36" (91.4 cm) piece of cheesecloth scrunched into a soft ball. Place the cheesecloth on the surface, lift slightly, and replace with a slight forward push.
Tip: This is really easy, but the motion does take practice. Avoid creating thin or heavy spots. Relax, and don't overwork the surface.

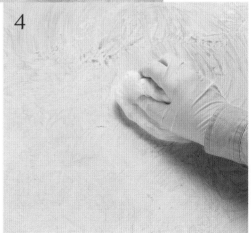

5 Topcoat with one or two coats of varnish.

Note: The wood insert at the top of page 68 was created with the paint colors listed in the materials list.

23 | Faux Marquetry

MARQUETRY IS THE craft of forming a decorative panel composed of shaped sections of wood veneer. It takes years to master that art, but you can easily simulate the look with stain on raw wood.

This simple yet elegant technique, appropriate for side panels and table-tops, makes an armoire's front doors stunning. Used in smaller scale on chests and boxes, the finish becomes a lovely, traditional detail (usually depicted in a half starburst or shell design).

This finish is usually done on wood, but you could certainly re-create the look of marquetry on other surfaces by combining it with *Basic Wood Graining* (page 88).

Refer to *Gel Stains* (page 13) and page 14 before beginning.

MATERIALS AND TOOLS

- ruler or tape measure
- pencil
- blue painter's tape, 1" (2.5 cm)
- gel stain, Old Masters®, Red Mahogany
- flat oil paintbrush, 1" (2.5 cm)
- T-shirt rags
- gel stain, Old Masters®, Dark Walnut
- gel stain, Old Masters®, Golden Oak

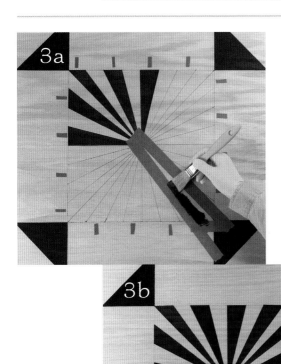

1 Mark off the design lightly with the pencil. The example shown is on a 16" (40.6 cm) square panel, but use any size surface, square or rectangular configuration, or any width border. Evenly mark off a 4" (10.2 cm) border on all sides to create four corner squares and a 14" (35.6 cm) inner square. Divide the small outer squares into two triangles.

Divide the center square into four triangles by drawing a line from corner to corner. Mark each side at 2" (5.1 cm) increments. Draw a line from each mark to the center point. **Tip:** For more or fewer inner triangles, divide the length of one side of the square by the desired number and mark at the appropriate inch marks.

2 Tape the edges of the four border triangles. Stain with mahogany using the 1" (2.5 cm) paintbrush. Soften the stain by wiping toward the centers with a soft rag, taking care not to lift the tape. Allow the stain to dry slightly, and then remove the tape.

3 Place a small piece of tape *outside* every other inner triangle. Tape off a marked triangle, press the tape firmly to secure it, and apply the walnut stain using the 1" (2.5 cm) paintbrush, following the procedure in step 2. Repeat for each triangle. Allow the stain to dry slightly and then remove all of the tape.

4 Tape, then apply oak stain to the remaining inner triangles and then the border area, following steps 2 and 3. Allow the stain to cure for 24 hours.

5 Topcoat the surface with one or two coats of varnish or wax.

ELEGANT AND EASY, this finish works well as an inlay on large tables or desktops. Leather hides tend to be smaller than 19" × 30" (48.3 × 76.2 cm), so inlays with dimensions smaller than that most successfully mimic real leather.

You may apply the *Faux Leather* finish to contemporary furniture pieces; however, when used where one might traditionally find leather inlays, the finish is more believable.

$\mathcal{24}$ Faux Leather

Color variations in tanned leather range from reddish Cordova to a deep brown/black, so although the library table shown was painted in brown tones, your choice of colors is open. You may experiment using latex paints and mediums to create this finish, but the oil glaze gives a richness that the latex just cannot quite achieve.

Refer to *Folding* (page 19) and pages 7, 8, and 14 before beginning.

MATERIALS AND TOOLS

- blue painter's tape, ½" (1.3 cm)
- painter's paper, 3" (7.6 cm) (optional)
- flat oil-based paint, golden brown
- flat oil-based paint, brown
- alkyd glazing liquid
- paint thinner
- flat oil paintbrush, 3" (7.6 cm)
- newspaper
- cheesecloth, 90-weight, 24" (61 cm)

1 You may apply the *Faux Leather* finish to the entire project piece, allowing the tape lines to form panels, or use 3" (7.6 cm) painter's paper to protect the outer surface to create an inlaid look. *Faux Leather* complements both painted and stained surfaces.

Basecoat the project or inlay surface with the golden brown paint or a color that is about 50 percent lighter than your glaze color. Apply the painter's tape, creating the desired inlay size. Press the tape firmly in place with your fingertips.
Tip: Using a clear ruler and a T-square keeps the tape lines straight.

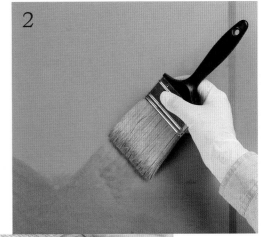

2 Mix a glaze using one-part brown paint, one-part glazing liquid, and one-part paint thinner. Apply the glaze to the entire project surface using the paintbrush.

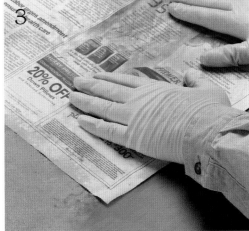

3 While the glaze is still wet, smoothly lay the sheet of newspaper onto the glazed surface. Keep the newspaper flat. Lift the newspaper; then replace it on the project surface overlapping the first area slightly and avoiding right angles. Repeat this process over the entire project or inlay surface. Begin step 4 while the glaze is still wet.

4 Soften some of the edge lines by patting with the smooth side of a cheesecloth wad. You just want to soften the lines and fold the texture into the finish. Allow the paint to dry; then remove the tape.

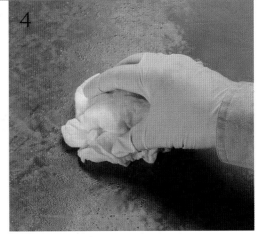

5 Topcoat the surface with one or two coats of wax. For greater protection, apply a satin oil-based varnish before waxing.

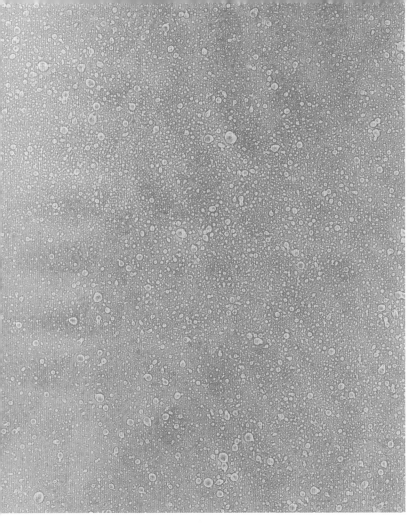

25 | Shagreen

SHAGREEN IS A high-end treated leather used on very special objects and furniture pieces. The roughened, untanned, and green-dyed leather once came from the hide on a horse's back. Shagreen is now commonly made of the skins from sharks and stingrays. You will create this lovely finish from paint, leaving all the sea life in peace.

Shagreen was traditionally prepared by embedding plant seeds in the soft, untreated hide. The hide was then covered with a cloth and trampled upon to push the seeds into the skin. When the skin dried, the seeds were shaken off leaving the leather peppered with small indentations.

Although used prior to it, the shagreen finish was very popular during the Art Nouveau era, so Art Deco styled furniture benefits from this finish. Still used today, shagreen is a beautiful finish on contemporary and traditional furniture.

Refer to pages 7, 8, and 14 before beginning.

MATERIALS AND TOOLS

- flat latex paint, linen white
- flat latex paintbrush, 3" (7.6 cm)
- flat oil-based paint, pale green/yellow
- alkyd glazing liquid
- mineral spirits
- flat oil paintbrush, 3" (7.6 cm)
- foam roller, 1" (2.5 cm)
- spray bottle with settings
- water

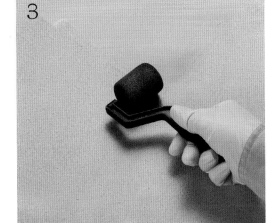

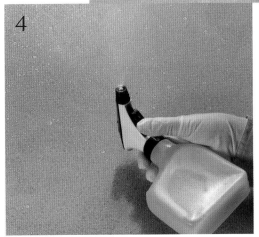

1 Basecoat the project surface with the linen white paint using the latex paintbrush. An optional basecoat color is a pale/light value steely/dirty gray.
Note: This technique is best created on a flat surface. Small projects must remain horizontal during the entire process. You may wish to basecoat a sample board and practice steps 2 to 4 before beginning to work on your project piece.

2 Mix a glaze using one-part green/yellow paint, one-part glazing liquid, and two-parts mineral spirits. Apply the glaze evenly to the entire surface using the oil paintbrush. If a gray basecoat was applied, use a medium dark steel-gray glaze.

3 Create a dimpled texture by rolling the foam roller in a random pattern over the wet glaze. Avoid over-rolling and work quickly so the glaze remains wet.

4 To create the distinctive spotted pattern, hold the water-filled spray bottle over the wet glaze, nozzle skyward, and spray straight up into the air. The falling water drops "break" the oil-based paint into circles. Spray over the entire project.

5 Adjust the nozzle to create larger circles and spray randomly. The completed surface will have mostly small circles with occasional larger circles. Allow the water to evaporate and the project surface to dry completely.

6 Topcoat the surface with one or two coats of oil varnish or wax.

26 | Faux Goatskin

THE SOFT LOOK of goatskin complements contemporary furniture and works beautifully on traditional pieces as an inlay. Typically goat hides are small, so similar shapes and sizes are pieced together to cover large areas. Scale the size of your torn paper pieces to fit your surface.

This finish is done with oil-based paint and Japan Color for three particular reasons. The edges of the sections get wiped out to create a "pieced-goatskin mark," the Japan Color raw

sienna and raw umber earth tones are the perfect shades for this finish, and they come premixed in convenient half-pints.

Plan to apply this finish to the entire surface in one session; the paint must not dry completely until you are finished. You may force-dry between steps with a hair dryer, but be careful not to overdry the area.

Refer to pages 7, 8, and 14 before beginning.

MATERIALS AND TOOLS

- flat latex paint, off-white
- latex paintbrush, 3" (7.6 cm)
- smooth, acid-free artist sketchbook pad, 18" × 24" (45.7 × 61 cm)

- flat oil-based paint, white
- flat oil paintbrush, 2" (5.1 cm)
- Japan Color, raw sienna
- Japan Color, raw umber
- cheesecloth, 90-weight

- oval sash paintbrush, 2" (5.1 cm)
- blue painter's tape, 1" (2.5 cm)
- paint thinner
- flat oil-based varnish or wax

1 Basecoat the project surface with off-white paint, using the latex paintbrush.

2 Tear several sheets of paper into graceful arcs or curves. Place the paper on the project surface, masking off a section. Hold down the edge you'll be painting off of with your hand.

Apply the white oil-based paint randomly using the oil paintbrush, painting off the paper's edge into the section. Wipe the paintbrush on a rag or paper towel, then repeat, using raw sienna and covering a smaller area. Repeat using the raw umber. **Tip:** Use the raw sienna and raw umber in different amounts within a section to simulate the unique coloration of each goatskin.

3 Continue to hold the paper in place and softly blend the colors with a cheesecloth wad.

4 Use the clean oval sash paintbrush to blend out the cheesecloth texture. Hold the paintbrush perpendicular to, and then pounce on, the surface. Softly swipe the paintbrush into the center occasionally to simulate the fur. Don't overdo this. Remove the paper and allow the section to dry, or force dry with a hair dryer, until the sheen becomes matte.

5 Repeat steps 2 to 4 to complete all sections. When creating a section that touches another, arrange the paper to very slightly expose the edges of the previously painted sections.

The oil-based paint lifts the paint from the previously painted hide, creating an outline. If the paint doesn't lift off easily, wipe from the edge of the paper onto the painted area, just enough to leave a join-line, with a cheesecloth slightly dampened with paint thinner.

6 Topcoat with one or two coats of varnish or wax.

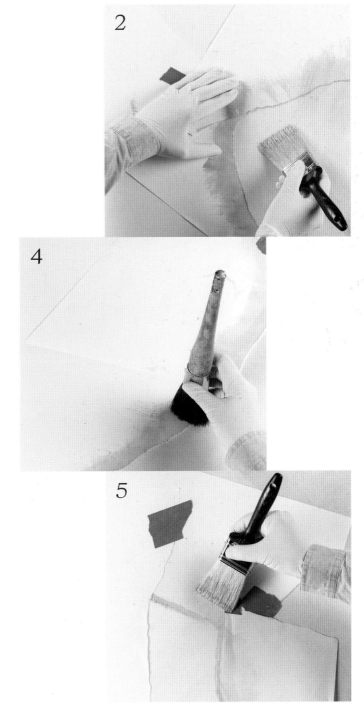

MALACHITE IS DELIGHTFUL on occasional tables and looks quite contemporary. Whether used alone or in combination with other faux stone techniques such as *Intarsia* (page 38) or with faux wood inlays, it presents a worldly richness and sophistication.

Use it on large surfaces for drama. The finish shown here simulates slab-cut malachite, which is often used on fine furniture. When you paint, you are re-creating the laying of the stone pieces, so draw obtuse angles and scale the size of the sections appropriately for the surface area.

You will also be re-creating with an eraser the multiple elongated oval curves that appear when malachite is sliced. You will want four patterns to avoid repetition and to avoid wear on the eraser.

27 | Malachite

Check the pattern by brushing paint on a piece of aluminum foil. Slice the eraser until you have a pattern you like.

In its raw form malachite is lumpily globular, a form called "botryoidal," (bah-tree-OYD-al) which means "grape cluster." It's a fun word to know and say.

The rippling ovals curve, forming a line that can be a tight or flattened arc. Just about anything goes (except forming round "bubbles"), so relax and have fun!

Refer to pages 7, 8, and 14 before beginning.

MATERIALS AND TOOLS

- eggshell latex paint, pale mint green
- latex paintbrush, 3" (7.6 cm)
- ruler
- pencil
- flat oil-based paint, deep rich green

- alkyd glazing liquid
- paint thinner
- white rubber eraser, notched
- craft knife
- aluminum foil
- blue painter's tape, 1" (2.5 cm)

- painter's paper, 3" (7.6 cm)
- flat oil paintbrush, 2" (5.1 cm)
- cheesecloth, 90-weight
- hair dryer (optional)
- gloss oil-based varnish

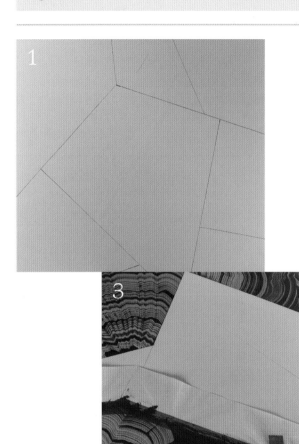

1 Basecoat the project surface with the latex paint using the latex paintbrush. Draw your inlay pattern using a pencil and the ruler. Avoid 90 degree angles.

2 Notch all four sides of a white rubber eraser with the craft knife.

3 Apply painter's tape along all the edges of a section, placing painter's paper along its outside edge. Mix a glaze using one-part oil-based paint, one-part glazing liquid, and one-part paint thinner. Brush the green glaze evenly over the section using the oil paintbrush. Gently pull your eraser over the "inside" of the section using a rippling motion to make curved and pointed parts of the first arc. Slightly twist the eraser occasionally to create an interesting pattern. Stop and restart without removing the eraser to emulate natural rock pressure lines.

Pull the next arc following the pattern, or leave voids, or change to another side of the eraser.

Allow the section to dry until the paint becomes matte, and then complete all of the sections. Vary the direction of the arcs from section to section. Allow the project to dry overnight.

4 Mix a stained overglaze with two-parts original glaze to one-part paint thinner. Brush over the entire surface, using the oil paintbrush, to create a more believable malachite texture and to reduce the contrast. Soften the glaze by patting with a wad of cheesecloth. Allow to dry overnight.

5 Topcoat with one or two coats of varnish.

Fabulous Fakes | 79

THE *FAUX STONE* finish offers a believable and quick way to create the look of stone without a lot of fuss and muss. The materials do the work for you.

There are many types of stone in the world—somewhere there is a natural stone that resembles the one in the finish described here! This finish offers you a basic approach to creating the appearance of stone. Select different colors or use multiple colors or even multiple applications of the techniques.

28 | Faux Stone

As with wood graining, the use of natural earth colors makes this finish say "stone."

The only "trick" to this technique is to avoid letting your glaze dry before you are satisfied with your result.

Refer to pages 7, 8, and 14 before beginning.

MATERIALS AND TOOLS

- flat latex paint, white
- flat latex paintbrush, 3" (7.6 cm)
- latex paint, light tan
- latex glazing liquid
- water
- two paint pails
- cheesecloth, 90-weight, 24" (61 cm)
- denatured alcohol
- oval sash paintbrush, 2" (5.1 cm)

1 Basecoat the project surface or inlay area with the white paint using the flat latex brush.

2 Mix a glaze using one-part tan paint, one-part glazing liquid, and one-part water (you may use any earth tone color latex paint in place of the tan). Brush over the entire surface using the latex paintbrush. The amount of water added to the glaze will vary the look—experiment to find a look you like. Dampen the cheesecloth with water and wring it out well. Texture most, but not all, of the glaze with the cheesecloth by pressing and lifting while the paint is still wet.

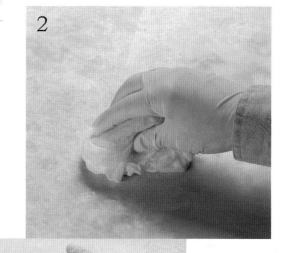

3 Pour a bit of denatured alcohol into a bowl. Dip your fingers into the alcohol. Hold them above the surface, then flick the alcohol. Repeat as many times as needed to create a variety of splatters, but avoid flooding the surface.
Note: The untexturized areas develop a more graphic look when splattered.

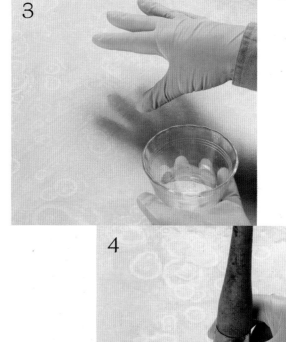

4 Hold the oval sash brush perpendicular to the surface, and pounce randomly to soften the contrast and to blend selected areas, while the paint and alcohol are still wet. Do not over-pounce.
Tip: If you do go too far and end up with a blur, allow the surface to dry, reapply the glaze and begin again.

5 Topcoat with one or two coats of varnish.

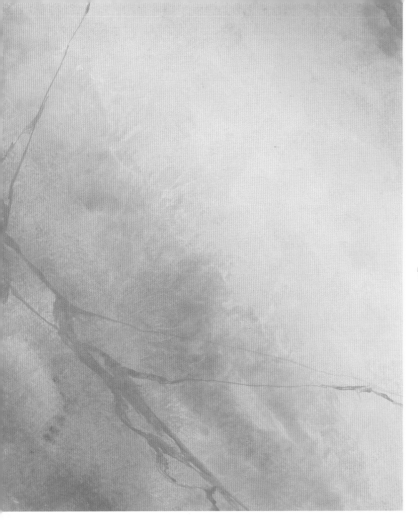

29 | Marble

THE SIMPLE TECHNIQUES used on this finish create a realistic marble, one that avoids looking overworked and clumsy, but appears effortless and elegant.

The following instructions detail how to achieve a basic and believable faux marble that you can apply to almost any surface.

Try combinations of colors: black with white, shades of gray, green with beige, or deep green with white. Keep your marble colors natural and you will create a finish that fools all who see your completed piece.

One of the tricks is to keep your paint movement following roughly a 45 degree angle (this is usually the pattern the earth produced when it formed certain marbles). Also, apply veining to less than 20 percent of the marble.

You will be applying three glazes, one after the other, and blending, so a quick touch will be helpful, as the paints must remain moist.

Refer to pages 7, 8, and 14 before beginning.

Tip: If you not feel confident enough to manipulate latex paint, use oil-based paints following the glazing recipe on page 12. Oil-based paint blends easily and offers a longer working time.

MATERIALS AND TOOLS

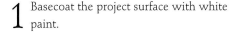

- flat latex paint, white
- flat latex paintbrush, 3" (7.6 cm)
- flat latex paint, beige
- flat latex paint, taupe
- latex glazing liquid

- water
- three paint pails
- cheesecloth, 90-weight
- turkey feather, white
- satin varnish

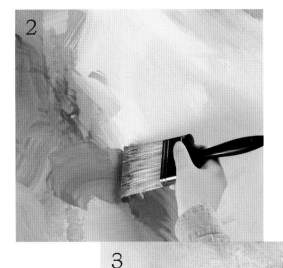

1 Basecoat the project surface with white paint.

2 Mix one-part paint, one-part glazing liquid, and one-part water to make the white, beige, and taupe glazes. Brush the white glaze in a 45 degree direction, covering about one-half of the surface. Wipe the paintbrush on a rag or paper towel; apply the beige glaze covering less than half of the surface. Blend the beige slightly into the white. Wipe the paintbrush; apply the taupe glaze covering one-fourth of the surface; blend some of the taupe into the other colors. Move to step 3 while the glazes are still wet.

3 Make a soft ball with a slightly water-dampened cheesecloth. Blend the three colors together leaving some of the cheesecloth texture in the paint. Allow the paint to dry.

4 The veining color is often slightly lighter than the darkest color; mix a bit of white glaze into the taupe.

Mix the veining paint to skim milk consistency with water. Dampen the feather with water, and then load it with the paint. Tickle the feather across the surface with a light pressure, pulling in a straight line. Form larger veins by laying the feather down and slightly rolling it. Keep the veins straight-sided, not scalloped or wiggly. Begin in the darkest area and pull through to other areas. Go off the edge or let the vein disappear. Avoid right angles and intersecting X-crossed veins. Blot the veins with cheesecloth as you work so they recede into the surface.

Tip: Practice veining on a sample board.

5 Topcoat with one or two coats of varnish.

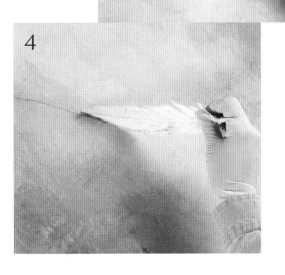

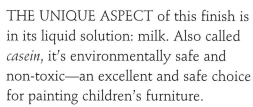

THE UNIQUE ASPECT of this finish is in its liquid solution: milk. Also called *casein*, it's environmentally safe and non-toxic—an excellent and safe choice for painting children's furniture.

Milk paint dries to an extremely flat sheen, producing a lovely antique look to country style furniture. It's associated with the Colonial period and with the Shaker community whose members still use it on their furniture. Don't limit this versatile finish to the expected styles though; it's perfect for island style and shabby chic.

The paint comes in a powder form and is mixed with water to make either a full-bodied or a thin, glaze-like paint. Follow the mixing directions that accompany the product, as different

30 | Shaker Finish

companies have slightly different mixing recipes. The paint comes in both soft pastel and strong rich colors.

There is a slight milky odor when it is applied, but it dries completely odorless. This paint will spoil, so mix only what you need. The leftover paint may be stored in the refrigerator for a few days.

This translucent finish is done over raw wood. The most beautiful topcoat for this paint is hand-rubbed wax, but topcoat with one or two coats of flat oil-based varnish to keep watermarks away. Follow the manufacturer's instructions if you use an acrylic topcoat.

MATERIALS AND TOOLS

- measuring cup, 1 pint (500 ml)
- water
- milk paint, Old Fashioned Milk Paint®, Snow White
- flat latex paintbrush, 3" (7.6 cm)
- sandpaper, 220-grit
- wax

1 Following the manufacturer's instructions, mix 6 oz (170 g) powdered paint into 1 pt (500 ml) of warm water. Allow the paint to rest for 10 to 15 minutes before applying it to the raw wood surface.

2 Apply the milk paint in the direction of the wood grain. Allow the paint to dry for at least one hour.

3 Apply a second coat. The coverage should look somewhat grainy. Allow the paint to dry for at least one hour.

4 Apply a third coat. This gives a transparency without visible brushstrokes. If you prefer, you may continue until the coverage is opaque. Allow to dry overnight; then sand smooth.

5 Topcoat with one or two coats of wax.

31 | Burled Wood

BURLS ARE THE gnarly and knotted warts found on trees. They are highly desired as veneers and for "highlight" panels on high-end furniture designed to showcase the uniqueness of the wood. They are often used to make boxes and clocks, as well as small turnings and bowls.

Burls are great fun because anything goes—grain crashes into itself and wild swirls meander across the surface. All this finish takes to be wonderful is a relaxed attitude! Enjoy the process and you will create a lovely burl. This is a great finish to try on a multiple caffé latte day, as squiggles and twitches make the best burl patterns.

As with any faux wood technique, the colors used say "wood" more than anything else.

Refer to *Universal Tinting Colorants* (page 11) and pages 7, 8, and 14 before beginning.

MATERIALS AND TOOLS

- eggshell latex paint, light tan
- flat latex paintbrush, 3" (7.6 cm)
- satin oil-based varnish

- flat oil paintbrush, 3" (7.6 cm)
- paint tray
- UTC, burnt umber
- UTC, raw umber

- gloves
- T-shirt rags
- satin oil-based varnish
- paint thinner (optional)

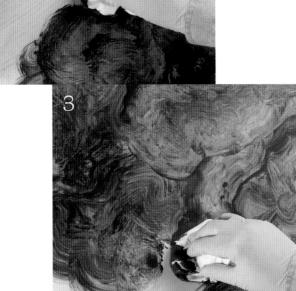

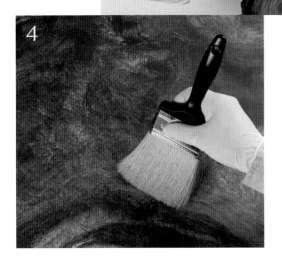

1 Basecoat the project surface with the light tan paint using the latex brush. This will be the lightest color in your burl. You may use another color if you prefer.

2 Brush a thick coat of varnish over a workable surface area with the oil paintbrush. (A workable area is indicated with tinted varnish in the example shown.) Pour a small puddle of burnt umber on the ridged, upper area of the paint tray. Pour a raw umber puddle next to, but not touching, the other UTC. Pour varnish in the trough portion. Wad the T-shirt rag into a small, loose ball.

Dip the rag into the burnt umber and then into the varnish. Smoosh the tip of the rag around on the varnished portion of the project surface, creating a ragged oval, an abstract shape, or a short, curved line. Use medium pressure, as if wiping up a spot of something. Squiggle the rag, pushing it with a nervous little twitch. If you miss a spot, pat color into the void.

3 Repeat the smooshing using a clean rag, varnish, and raw umber.

Develop a radial (sunburst) pattern as you work back and forth using both colors. Create more burls with burnt umber than with raw umber. If the varnish on the project surface begins to dry out, apply a bit more with a rag. If the drying is accelerated by hot, dry air, dip the rag into a small amount of paint thinner occasionally.

4 Dry-brush lightly, moving the oil paintbrush in a radial pattern, from the center of a "burl" outward to simulate a growth pattern. The varnish will be wet and tacky, so wipe the paintbrush on a dry cloth now and then.

5 Topcoat with one or two coats of varnish.

TWO THINGS CREATE realistic wood: color and grain. Using the basic techniques of combing, ragging, and flogging, you can create grain to simulate almost any type of wood. Beautiful on its own, this finish also works well as an accent border with the other finishes in this book.

Although not a furniture piece, doors (both steel and painted) are a wonderful surface for wood graining. If working on a door with inset panels, be sure to follow what would have been the natural direction of the wood grain.

32 | Basic Wood Graining

You can find many specialty brushes and tools on the market to produce wood graining, and while they are wonderful tools, the only two you ever really need are a good flogger brush, and a set of steel combs.

To achieve the proper finish color, start with the proper basecoat color. If you are trying to match an existing wood, the basecoat paint must match the lightest color of the wood. Use an eggshell sheen for the basecoat, whether latex or oil-based.

Oil-based varnish is used for wood graining, as its longer drying time is forgiving and simple to erase with mineral spirits should a mistake happen.

Refer to pages 7, 8, and 14 before beginning.

- eggshell latex paint, Benjamin Moore Paints #1047 Aquavelvet
- flat latex paintbrush, 3" (7.6 cm)
- measuring cup, 1 pint (500 ml)
- satin oil varnish, clear
- paint pail
- UTC, burnt umber
- UTC, raw umber
- UTC, raw sienna
- chip brush, 3" (7.6 cm)
- steel wood graining combs (these usually are sold in a set)
- T-shirt rags
- flogger brush

Note: A chip brush is an inexpensive, rough-bristled paintbrush

1 Basecoat the project surface with latex paint using the latex paintbrush.

Translucent, tinted varnish is the medium for *Basic Wood Graining*. Pour 1 pint (500 ml) of varnish into the paint pail. Drip small amounts of all three UTC colors into the varnish slowly until you create a color you like (start with about three-parts burnt umber, two-parts raw umber, and one-part raw sienna). You may need to add more colorant to make enough solution for large pieces, but continue slowly; if too much colorant is added, it will float and not mix, and the varnish will never dry.

Tip: The colorant never dries; wipe up spills immediately or it can spread everywhere.

2 Repetitive raking creates a realistic wood grain. Apply tinted varnish in the direction of the grain using a chip brush. Rake a comb back and forth quickly, multiple times, from top to bottom until a grain pattern emerges.

3 Pull a soft T-shirt rag from top to bottom, jittering the motion slightly, to create a vaguely rippled linear pattern. The wrinkly line creates a very believable wood grain.

4 Hold the flogger brush parallel to the surface, bristles downward. Slap the surface with quick snaps, working from the top down. Flog the entire surface a couple of times until you are satisfied with the look. Allow to dry for 24 hours.

Tip: Real wood grain never crashes into itself, so your grain lines need to run parallel to each another.

5 Topcoat with one or two coats of varnish.

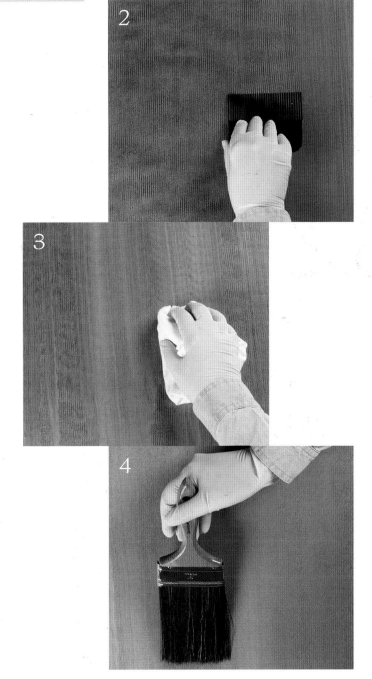

33 | Mahogany

IN THIS TECHNIQUE color makes the finish believable. Mahogany serves as a beautiful finish for tabletops and inset side panels, and makes an inferior wood piece a superior one.

Mahogany is a quiet wood; the grain is fine, and what grain you see is fairly straight-lined without knots or whirls. It's also an elegant wood, and this finish should be selected for use on stylish furniture pieces.

Mahogany goes beyond *Basic Wood Graining* through its deeper basecoat color, the addition of Venetian red UTC to the graining varnish, and an additional paintbrush technique.

Refer to *Basic Wood Graining* (page 88) and pages 7, 8, and 14 before beginning.

MATERIALS AND TOOLS

- eggshell latex paint, Benjamin Moore #1048 Aquavelvet
- flat latex paintbrush, 3" (7.6 cm)
- measuring cup, 1 pint (500 ml)
- satin oil-based varnish, clear
- paint pail

- UTC, burnt umber
- UTC, raw umber
- UTC, Venetian red
- chip brush, 3" (7.6 cm)
- T-shirt rags
- flogger brush

- chip brush, 1½" (3.8 cm)
- steel wood graining combs (usually sold in a set)

Note: A chip brush is an inexpensive, somewhat rough-bristled paintbrush.

1 Basecoat the project surface with latex paint using the latex paintbrush.

Translucent, tinted varnish is the graining medium for *Mahogany*. Pour 1 pint (500 ml) of varnish into the paint pail. Drip small amounts of all three UTC colors into the varnish slowly until you create a color you like (start with about three-parts burnt umber, two-parts raw umber, and one-part Venetian red). You may need to add more colorant to make enough solution for large pieces, but continue slowly; if too much colorant is added, it will float and not mix, and the varnish will never dry.

Tip: The colorant never dries; wipe up spills immediately or it can spread everywhere.

2 Apply the graining varnish with the large chip brush using a straight top-to-bottom stroke. Texture the varnish by lightly pulling a soft T-shirt rag over the surface from top to bottom. Jitter the motion slightly to create a vaguely rippled linear pattern. The wrinkly line creates a very believable mahogany grain. Repeat over the entire surface.

3 Hold the flogger brush parallel to the surface, bristles downward. Slap the surface with quick snaps, working from the top down. Flog the entire surface to soften the rag marks.

4 Dip the tip of the small chip brush into the graining varnish. Hold it at a 45 degree angle to the grain and lay in a dark accent by dragging the chisel-edge down the entire length of the grain. Use this accent sparingly, perhaps one per side. Allow to dry for 24 hours.

5 Topcoat with one or two coats of varnish.

34 | Rust

THIS FINISH MAY SHOW a heavy corrosion, or the beginning of rust formation. The example shown here signifies the earlier stage. Apply more of the yellowish and burnt orange paints to make a rustier looking surface.

This is a great look for patio furniture, interior occasional tables, and objects such as urns for both inside and outside.

Refer to pages 7, 8, and 14 before beginning.

MATERIALS AND TOOLS

- latex antique bronze paint, Modern Masters® Antique Bronze, ME 204 (opaque)
- latex paintbrush, 3" (7.6 cm)
- flat latex paint, black/brown
- natural sea sponge
- T-shirt rags
- latex glazing liquid
- flat latex paint, brick red
- flat latex paint, earthy yellow
- water
- water-based varnish, Modern Master® Dead Flat

1 Basecoat the project surface with the antique bronze paint using the latex paintbrush.

2 Apply the black/brown paint, covering the entire surface. Apply this paint so it is thicker in some areas and thinner in others (sloppily). Allow it to dry to the matte stage, but not to dry completely.

3 Dab a wet sea sponge over the barely dry paint with one hand, and remove the black paint with a T-shirt rag in the other hand. Work back and forth until the antique bronze shows through on most of the surface. You may have to scrub at the paint a bit, but if it hasn't dried completely, it will come off.

4 Mix four-parts glazing liquid, four-parts paint, and one-part water to make both the brick red and the yellow glazes.

    Brush the yellow glaze over 75 percent of the surface using the dampened sea sponge. Rinse the sponge, press to remove the excess water, and apply the red glaze over 60 percent of the surface.

    Blend and soften the glazes with a water-dampened T-shirt rag. In some places the two will meld into a warm orangey color. Some of the antique bronze color should show through here and there. Leave heavier glaze deposits over the black/brown paint areas. Allow to dry.

Note: Either glaze may be sparingly sponged over the surface to create a depth to the rust that you like.

5 Topcoat with one or two coats of varnish.

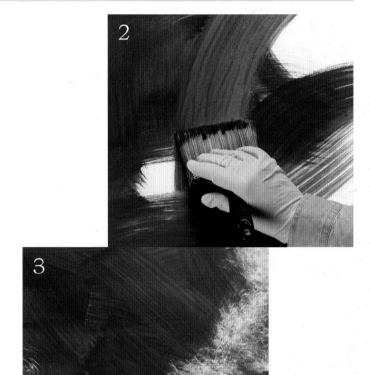

35 | Bronze

BRONZE IS A copper and tin alloy. The color may look similar to the verdigris copper, owing to the copper content in bronze. This finish emulates the color of bronze statuary. Bronze generally receives a chemical patina to maintain the deep luster of the newly made casting. If you study photos of bronzes, you will find a wide range of coloration.

This finish demonstrates what happens when "incompatible" paints work together. The application method is unique: latex paint applied over metallic paint, which makes it separate and crawl over the surface. Ordinarily this is bad, but on this finish, it is good.

Refer to *Folding* and *French Brush* (page 19), and pages 7 and 8 before beginning.

- spray paint, Rust-oleum American Accents® Designer Metallic
- two paint pails
- water
- semigloss latex paint, black
- flat latex paintbrush, 3" (7.6 cm)
- cheesecloth, 90-weight
- hair dryer (optional)
- dull or satin oil varnish

1 Basecoat the project surface solidly with the spray paint. Pour water into one pail, and black paint into the other as soon as the basecoat dries to the touch. Dip the paintbrush 1" (2.5 cm) into the black paint; then dip the loaded paintbrush into the water and thinly apply the paint to the surface using the French brush technique.

2 Fold in the black paint with a cheesecloth pad. Allow this layer to dry to the touch or force-dry with a hair dryer. The surface will look mostly bronze at this point.

3 Continue to build up semitransparent layers by repeating steps 1 and 2. You want to see the metallic bronze under the black, but have the finish softly obliterating it.

4 Topcoat with one or two coats of varnish.

WEATHERED AND AGED copper acquires a beautiful natural patina—one that is very easy to duplicate. There are many patina kits on the market that have pre-mixed colors. While they are good, there never seems to be enough to do a large furniture piece. This technique will allow you to work on entire patio sets, tabletops of any size, and even cabinetry.

There are also many good copper spray paints on the market. Use any you like for the copper basecoat, following the manufacturer's instructions.

36 Verdigris Patina

You may also use one of the pre-mixed, water-based copper metallic paints.

A chemical reaction created by the atmosphere causes the copper to turn green. It "blooms" slowly (transparently), growing almost opaque. Areas of transparency and heavier blue/green glaze lend a realistic air to the finish.

Refer to *Dry Brush* (page 19) and to pages 7, 8, and 14 before beginning.

MATERIALS AND TOOLS

- spray paint, Rust-oleum® Bright Copper
- flat latex paint, warm black/brown
- latex glazing liquid
- water
- three paint pails
- two flat latex paint-brushes, 4" (10.2 cm)
- T-shirt rags
- flat latex paint, blue/green
- flat latex paint, white
- water-based varnish, Modern Masters® Dead Flat

1 Basecoat the project surface with the spray paint.

2 Mix a glaze using four-parts black/brown paint, four-parts glazing liquid, and one-part water. Brush the glaze quickly over the entire surface, using one of the latex paint-brushes. Wipe out the center with the T-shirt rag. Do not allow the paint to dry.

3 Dry-brush the wet paint using the clean latex paintbrush, to soften and blend. Wipe the paintbrush on a rag to clean for use in step 4. Allow to dry.

4 Mix one-part paint, one-part glazing liquid, and one-part water to make the blue and the white glazes. Brush the blue glaze over the entire surface. Immediately brush white glaze over 10 percent of the blue. Wipe out the center with a clean T-shirt rag. Dry-brush to soften. Allow to dry.

5 Topcoat with one or two coats of varnish.

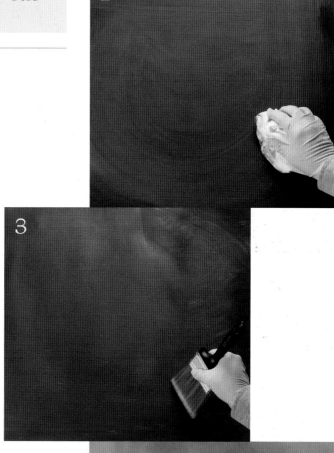

LAPIS IS THE Latin word for stone; the Persian word Lazhward, means blue; apparently at some point these two words came together. Although lapis lazuli (gem lapis) is better known, provincial lapis is more common. Gem lapis is the lightest, most consistently colored portion of lapis. Provincial lapis is used for most furniture inlay because

37 | Provincial Lapis

of its availability, greater color movement, and interesting depth. It is the lapis form used in this finish.

A stunning way to introduce the rich, deep, mysterious color of blue into any environment, it's beautiful on small, modern and contemporary occasional tables.

Refer to pages 7, 8, and 14 before beginning.

MATERIALS AND TOOLS

- flat latex or spray paint, gold
- flat latex paintbrush, 3" (7.6 cm)
- Japan Color, cobalt blue
- Japan Color, Prussian blue
- alkyd glazing liquid

- paint thinner
- flat oil paintbrush, 3" (7.6 cm)
- oval sash brush, 2" (5.1 cm)
- cheesecloth, 90-weight (optional)
- particle/dust mask

- metallic powder, rich gold
- satin oil-based varnish

Note: If you cannot find the Japan Color cobalt or Prussian blues, you may substitute by using artist's tube paint.

1 Basecoat the project surface with the gold paint and allow it to dry.

2 Mix one-part paint, one-part glazing liquid, and one-part paint thinner to make the two blue glazes. Slip-slap the cobalt glaze randomly over two or three areas of the project surface, using the flat oil paintbrush. Slip-slap the open areas with the Prussian blue glaze.

3 Firmly pounce with the sash brush, holding it perpendicularly to the surface, and moving at a 45 degree angle. This will blend the two colors together. If you would like more gold to show through, pat a few places with a cheesecloth, and then use the sash brush to remove the rag texture. Move to the next step while the paint is wet.

4 Do not inhale the powder; put the particle mask on before opening the powder.
  Place 1 tablespoon (15 ml) of gold powder into the center of a 6" (15.2 cm) square of cheesecloth, and fold. Hold your hand about 4 ft (1.2 m) above the surface and lightly tap the cheesecloth with your finger. The powder will float down onto surface. Fan your hand below the powder so it doesn't fall straight down onto the surface. Continue to apply the powder until you like the look.

5 This step is optional but adds a subtle variation. Pounce some of the powdered areas with the sash brush to produce a green accent. Do this sparingly, and follow the 45 degree movement.

6 Topcoat with one or two coats of varnish.

Antiquing
AND GILDING

38 | Stain Antiquing

ADD EXTRA PUNCH to simple stain-ing with this easy to accomplish finish. Apply *Stain Antiquing* over a freshly stained surface, or enhance a previously stained piece of wood or cabinetry. When working on an older or already stained piece, wash the surface well and allow it to dry thoroughly before you begin.

Refer to *All About Stains*, *Safety Procedures*, and *Safety Caution* (page 13), and pages 7, 8, and 14 before beginning.

MATERIALS AND TOOLS

- gel stain, Old Masters®, Golden Oak
- flat oil paintbrush, 1" (2.5 cm)
- T-shirt rags
- gel stain, Old Masters®, Dark Walnut

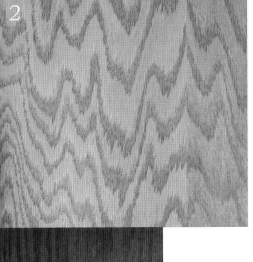

1 Dip a rag into the oak stain and apply using a circular motion. Use the small paintbrush to reach into corners or crevices.

2 Wipe the excess stain off with a clean rag. Allow to dry.

3 Apply the walnut stain to the edges and corners of the project surface; leave a clear oval area in the center. Wipe the stain into the center with a clean rag until the entire surface is antiqued.

4 Topcoat with one or two coats of varnish.

39 Staining and Distressing

OKAY, THIS IS the finish that allows you to vent all your pent-up frustrations! You get to beat, scrape, scratch, and otherwise destroy a surface. Everything you were ever taught about how not to hurt furniture is turned around and used when distressing a surface.

The beauty of age attracts us. Distressed furniture is like an old friend with signs of a life well lived; it shows years of service and use.

Natural wear happens in some places more than others, such as edges, around door handles, on legs and corners. With this in mind, decide where wear would likely occur on your surface, and attack it.

Common household items do the job, but go ahead and get inventive. Do enjoy creating beauty with imperfection.

Refer to *All About Stains, Safety Procedures*, and *Safety Caution* (page 13), *Distressing and Aging, Techniques and Tools* (pages 20 to 21), and pages 7, 8, and 14 before beginning. Also refer to *Cleaning* (page 16) if the surface has been previously stained.

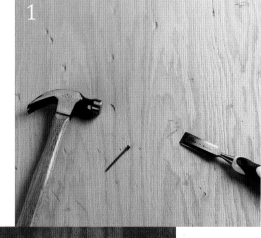

1 Clean old surfaces before beginning. Pound the project surface with both ends of the hammer to dent the wood, tap holes with the nail, or lay the nail on its side and pound for an interesting dent. Gouge large scrapes with the chisel by running it along one edge of the metal ruler. Distress corners with the hammer or chisel. Just have fun and mess it up.

2 Dip a rag into the oak stain and apply it to the center of the project surface using a circular motion. Apply the walnut stain along the edges, in recesses, cracks, and dents with a clean rag. Don't bother being neat. Use the small paintbrush to reach into corners or crevices.

3 Soften and blend the stains with a rag. Add more age by wiping the surface with a dirty rag to leave a deposit of heavier stain here and there. Your aim is to achieve a look of age, dirt, and a worn surface. Allow to dry.

4 Topcoat with one or two coats of varnish.

40 | Distressed Latex

WHAT A GREAT finish for raw wood furniture or those "must have" garage sale pieces. This finish may be applied over well-cleaned previously stained or varnished wood.

This is perfect for the country look and especially appropriate in children's rooms, as use and abuse enhances this finish. Furniture finished this way tends to have a New England seaside look.

Use your favorite colors to complement or contrast with other furniture or the room in which your surface will live.

Refer to *All About Stains, Safety Procedures, Safety Caution* (page 13), and *Hammer* (page 20), and pages 7, 8, and 14 before beginning. Also refer to *Cleaning* (page 16) if the surface has been previously stained.

MATERIALS AND TOOLS

- hammer
- flat latex paint, blue
- flat latex paintbrush, 4" (10.2 cm)
- flat latex paint, linen white
- T-shirt rag
- denatured alcohol
- gel stain, Old Masters®, Dark Walnut

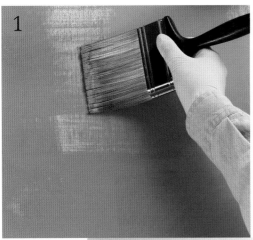

1 Clean old surfaces before beginning. If your furniture piece isn't already nicked and dinged, distress it with the hammer. Apply the blue paint, leaving some bare areas in the middle, the corners, and edges. Allow to dry.

2 Apply the white paint, covering the blue in the center of the surface, but leaving some blue paint and a few bare spots showing on the edges and corners. Allow the paint to dry to the matte stage, then dip a T-shirt rag into denatured alcohol and rub away some of the white paint, leaving a slightly patchy look. Also soften any brushstrokes. Allow to dry completely.

3 Dip a rag into the stain and apply it using a circular motion. Let the stain remain in dents and nicks, and leave a heavier deposit at the edges and corners. Soften the stain with a clean rag.

4 Topcoat with one or two coats of flat varnish or wax.

THIS IS ONE of the loveliest ways to antique a furniture piece. It's appropriate for just about any style and period. The graceful and soft finish can make a piece of furniture stand out or blend into an environment.

41 | Oil Paint Antiquing

Old, worn, or overly dark pieces of furniture with lovely lines or shape can be rescued with this finish. You will be amazed how that dresser or table you thought outdated and boring comes alive and looks like a whole new piece.

Refer to *Cleaning* (page 16), *Dry Brush* and *Pounce* (page 19) *Universal Tinting Colorants* (page 11) and pages 7, 8, and 14 before beginning.

MATERIALS AND TOOLS

- flat latex paint, white
- flat latex paintbrush, 4" (10.2 cm)
- flat oil-based paint, beige
- flat oil-based paint, green
- alkyd glazing liquid
- mineral spirits
- flat oil paintbrush, 3" (7.6 cm)
- cheesecloth, 90-weight
- UTC, burnt umber
- oil-based varnish

1 Clean old surfaces before beginning. Remove any drawer pulls or other hardware. Base-coat the project surface with the latex paint using the latex paintbrush. Allow to dry.

2 Mix one-part oil-based paint, one-part glazing liquid, and one-part mineral spirits to make the beige and green glazes. Apply the beige glaze with the oil paintbrush and wipe out the center with a piece of cheesecloth. Do not allow the glaze to dry.
Note: Complete all the steps on one side before moving to another side.

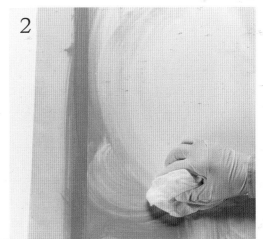

3 Dry-brush using the oil paintbrush to soften the glaze, then pounce slightly, using the same paintbrush, to soften the dry-brushed strokes.

4 Apply the green glaze with the oil paintbrush. Drag a cheesecloth rag through the glaze lightly from side to side to create some interest. Dry-brush gently with the latex brush to soften the pull strokes and blend the glaze. Allow to dry for 24 hours.

5 Mix the burnt umber into the varnish and brush over the entire piece using the oil paintbrush to further simulate age. The tinted varnish affects the colors, especially the green, turning it into a far more "mysterious" hue.

6 Topcoat with one or two coats of oil-based varnish.

42 Aluminum Gilding

ALL SEMI-PRECIOUS metal leaf types—copper, aluminum, and composition (imitation gold)—are applied following the same procedure, so use the leaf you prefer following the instructions for this finish.

A gilded surface, the most elegant and sophisticated of all the finishes, is the look that all the metallic paints and powders attempt to emulate. It's the real McCoy.

Good preparation of your furniture piece is all-important, as your gilding will only be as beautiful as your prep. Leaf covers nothing—it reveals everything.

Leaf sticks to a material called "gold size," which comes to the proper tack (stickiness) after a certain amount of time. If you apply the leaf when the gold size is too wet, you will "flood" the leaf and it will look grainy and awful. If you apply the leaf when gold size is too dry, the leaf will have skips (areas where the leaf doesn't adhere). To tell when gold size has reached the proper tack, put a knuckle to the surface and pull it away. You should feel a tight pull.

The best gold sizes are oil-based, as they level out beautifully. A "quick" gold size, fine for small projects, comes

& Copper Gilding 43

to tack in about an hour and stays at tack for about an hour. For medium to large projects, use a 12-hour gold size; it comes to the proper tack after about 12 to 13 hours and stays at tack for 6 to 12 hours.

Copper, aluminum, and composition leaf come in packages of 500 sheets consisting of 20 books with 25 sheets each. The cost varies depending on the type of metal, but purchase from a gilding supply store to get the best price, or check online.

Caution: Once you learn how to apply leaf to a surface—because the process is so wonderful and the results so beautiful—you might develop "Gilding Fever," an overwhelming desire to gild everything in sight.

Keep gilded items away from excessive heat and humidity, which can damage the gilding.

Refer to *Tufbacking* (page 18) and pages 7, 8, and 14 before beginning.

Note: Apply the gold size in a very well-ventilated area, as it has strong fumes. However, everything sticks to gold size, so avoid dusty or wind-blown areas.

- low-sheen oil-based enamel or spray paint, taupe or brick red
- flat oil paintbrush, 3" (7.6 cm)
- wet/dry sandpaper, 400-grit
- 12-hour gold size, Mixton A Dorer LaFranc®
- metal leaf, aluminum or copper
- tamper brush, 2" (5.1 cm)
- oil-based varnish

1 Basecoat the project surface with three coats of the appropriate enamel paint color, allowing the paint to dry between coats. Allow the final coat to dry for 24 hours, then tufback. The surface must be smooth and nonporous.
Note: The traditional basecoat color for copper and composition leaf is brick red. For aluminum it is medium grey or taupe.

2 Apply the gold size very thinly, stretching out the size with the flat paintbrush. Keep the coverage consistent and even.

3 Leaf is thinner than tissue paper and very delicate. The biggest trick to gilding is getting the fragile sheets to lie down; even a slight puff of wind wreaks havoc, so work in a protected area. Do not worry about skips; just relax and cover the surface. If you have difficulty gilding on a horizontal surface, turn the piece vertically, as gravity helps a bit.

Copper and composition leaf tarnish if touched. Although aluminum does not, handle all leaf in the same manner. Each piece of leaf comes between two pieces of paper; use them to handle and protect the leaf.

Hold the book of leaf in your hand, roll back the lower covering paper, and place the leaf over the surface. Set the top and gently move the book away, allowing the leaf to settle into place.

4 Move to the right and place the second sheet overlapping the first by barely ¼" (6 mm). Continue gilding, moving to the right. After completing one row, move down and apply the following row, "typewriter" style. Once you have covered the entire surface, fill in any skips.
Note: In the example shown, the papers covering the leaf have been rolled back to expose the leaf. Handle your leaf this way for good placement control, for once the leaf comes in contact with the surface, you are committed.

5 Tamp (smooth) down the leaf by softly brushing over, not against, the seams and the entire surface with the tamper brush. This ensures all the leaf is attached to the surface. Clean off all skewings (excess leaf) by dusting with the brush. Allow to dry overnight before tarnishing or varnishing.

6 Topcoat with one or two coats of varnish.
Note: Never apply tape of any sort to a gilded surface, even if varnished, as the leaf will lift.
Note: Never touch leaf with your hands. Your body oils will tarnish it.

44 | Carved Surface Gilding

WRAP YOUR REFLECTION in the warm glow of gold on a mirror frame or watch the radiance of light against gold on candle or wall sconces. Always an elegant touch, gold also adds warmth and a feeling of well-being.

Gilding on a carved surface takes a bit more care than gilding on a flat project surface, but the compensation surpasses the effort.

You must take care to avoid size pooling in the recesses. Use the stiff-bristled artist's paintbrush to remove any excess size.

If you have difficulty gilding on a horizontal surface, turn the piece vertically, as gravity helps a bit.

Refer to *Aluminum Gilding* and *Copper Gilding* (pages 110 to 113, *Tufbacking* (page 18), and to pages 7, 8, and 14 before beginning.

MATERIALS AND TOOLS

- low-sheen oil-based enamel or spray paint, brick red

- flat oil paintbrush, 3" (7.6 cm)

- steel wool, fine-grade

- wet/dry sandpaper, 400-grit (optional)

- 12-hour gold size, Mixton A Dorer LaFranc®

- short flat/bright artist's hog bristle paintbrush, 1" (2.5 cm)

- composition leaf

- very soft bristle* tamper or blending brush, 2" (5.1 cm)

- satin oil-based varnish

Note: *A badger hair paintbrush is best.

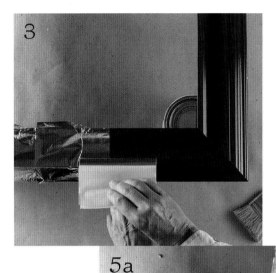

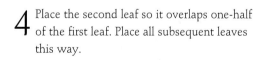

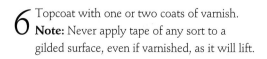

1 Apply three coats of enamel paint; allow the paint to dry between coats. After the third coat, allow the paint to dry for 24 hours. Lightly rub the entire surface with the steel wool (if your surface is flat enough to tufback, use that sanding method). Wipe lightly with a tack cloth to remove any grit. The surface must be smooth and nonporous.

2 Apply the gold size very thinly, stretching out the size with the brush. Keep the coverage consistent and even.

3 Leaf is thinner than tissue paper and very delicate. The biggest trick to gilding is getting the fragile sheets to lie down; even a bare puff of wind wreaks havoc, so work in a protected area. Do not worry about skips; just relax and cover the surface.

Hold the book of composition leaf in your hand, and place the first leaf over the surface. Set the top and gently move the book away, allowing the leaf to settle into place. Never touch the leaf with your fingers, as this causes tarnishing.

4 Place the second leaf so it overlaps one-half of the first leaf. Place all subsequent leaves this way.

5 Tamp down the leaf by softly brushing over, not against, the seams and over the entire surface. This ensures that all of the leaf is attached to the surface. Clean off all skewings by gently "dusting" with the brush. Allow to dry overnight before tarnishing or varnishing.

6 Topcoat with one or two coats of varnish. **Note:** Never apply tape of any sort to a gilded surface, even if varnished, as it will lift.

THIS FINISH BEGINS with a successfully gilded, but unvarnished, surface. The application method for composition leaf, the base for creating *Tarnished Patina*, is the same as that for aluminum leaf and copper leaf.

If you like the look of copper gilding, try the tarnishing process on the copper leaf. The results will be slightly different, but just as remarkable. Aluminum leaf will not tarnish.

Composition leaf tarnishes easily, so it requires careful handling until it is sealed. The plus side to its delicate nature means you can purposefully tarnish it to achieve some attention-grabbing results.

45 | Tarnished Patina

Traditionally, chemicals are used to create the tarnish. This finish employs a safer alternative—an everyday household product—white distilled vinegar.

Even though you will be applying a tarnish, the tarnish resulting from fingers is not desirable, so never touch the leaf with your hands until it is sealed.

Refer to *Tufbacking* (page 18), *Copper Gilding* (page 110 to 113), and pages 7, 8, and 14 before beginning.

Tip: It is the nature of tarnishing that you will never achieve the exact same result twice, so if you are trying to match two or more pieces, tarnish them at the same time.

MATERIALS AND TOOLS

- spray paint, Rust-oleum® "American Accents" Colonial Red or any orangish brick red
- wet/dry sandpaper, 400-grit
- sandpaper, 400- and 600-grit wet/dry
- 12-hour gold size, Mixton A Dorer LaFranc®
- composition leaf
- tamper brush, 2" (5.1 cm)
- white distilled vinegar
- glass measuring cup
- glass bowl
- badger or very soft natural bristle paintbrush, 3" (7.6 cm)
- T-shirt rags
- spray bottle with "mist" setting
- oil-based varnish

1 Basecoat the project surface with red paint, tufback and clean; gild the surface with composition leaf, tamp, and clean away all skewings.

2 Mix 1 cup (250 ml) of vinegar and ⅓ cup (75 ml) of water in a glass bowl. Dip the paintbrush in the vinegar mix, then pounce it on the leafed surface. Avoid brushing, which will leave marks. Move over the entire surface, but don't rework any area.

   The "tarnishing" appears after 45 minutes. Blot (do not rub) any remaining vinegar with a rag. Be very careful, as the leaf is "imperiled" at this point and you do not want to lift it.

3 Apply undiluted vinegar following the same application procedure as in step 2. Check on the surface after about an hour. When you like the amount of red showing through, stop the tarnishing process by misting the entire surface with water and blotting carefully with a rag. Allow to dry overnight.

4 Topcoat with one or two coats of oil-based varnish in any sheen. Do not use water-based or spray varnishes; they contain agents that will tarnish the leaf in an unwanted manner.
Note: Never apply tape of any sort to a gilded surface, even if varnished, as the leaf will lift.

46 | Noton

NOTON IS A Japanese form of broken leaf gilding. The color play between the dark basecoat and the leaf create a visually intriguing composition. The organic nature of a broken application makes the contrast between the glimmer of gold and the inkiness of the black surface doubly interesting.

Balance is important to achieve the overall grace of *Noton*. Distribute the leaf so it covers at least 80 percent of the basecoat, or be understated and go for 20 percent leaf coverage.

Refer to *Copper Gilding* (pages 110 to 113), *Tufbacking* (page 18), and pages 7, 8, and 14 before beginning.

MATERIALS AND TOOLS

- low-sheen oil-based enamel or spray paint, black
- flat oil paintbrush, 3" (7.6 cm)
- wet/dry sandpaper, 400-grit
- 12-hour gold size, Mixton A Dorer LaFranc®
- composition leaf
- wax paper
- tamper brush, 2" (5.1 cm)
- mineral spirits
- lint-free rag
- oil-based satin varnish

1 Apply three coats of black paint, allowing the paint to dry between coats. After the third coat, allow the paint to dry for 24 hours, then tufback. The surface must be smooth and nonporous.

2 Apply the gold size very thinly, stretching out the size with the flat paintbrush. Keep the coverage consistent and even. Allow the size to come to tack.

3 Drag the leaf over the surface. Tear the leaf into interesting shapes and sizes, and if you have them, use the skewings (excess leaf) saved from other gilding projects. Avoid right angles as you work. Use wax paper to press the leaf down so you can check your composition, or simply let it happen. The examples show the application progression.

4 Carefully tamp all leaf into place. If you have very small areas, place wax paper over the surface before tamping, but lift it immediately.

5 Dampen the rag with mineral spirits and carefully clean off the exposed size. Allow the surface to dry overnight.

6 Topcoat the surface with varnish even if some remaining size is still slightly tacky. Apply to an area only once; do not overbrush. Allow to dry. Apply at least two more coats of varnish, allowing each to dry between coats. Tufback to smooth out any roughness from the leaf before applying the final varnish coat.

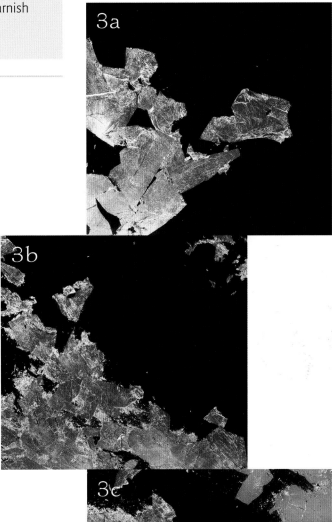

3a

3b

3c

47 | Antiqued Gold

THIS VERSATILE AND easy-to-do finish creates beautiful results. It's appropriate for just about any piece of furniture or object, for the interior or exterior. You will move from step to step while the paint is wet, making this a quick and simple finish.

For finishing pieces to be used outside, select exterior paints, and follow the manufacturer's instructions.

There are many gold paints on the market: metallic or flat in spray or brush-on form, and in oil-based and latex formulas. Use the paint most convenient to you, but spray paint gives a smoother finish.

This finish must be done on a flat, horizontal surface. Vertical surfaces must be laid flat. If your surface has small legs, pounce the black paint on and rag off to coordinate with the flat areas.

Refer to *Pouncing* (page 19) and pages 7, 8, and 14 before beginning.

- latex paint, gold
- flat latex paintbrush, 3" (7.6 cm)
- flat latex paint, warm black
- paint pail
- water
- cheesecloth, 90-weight
- terry cloth rags
- varnish

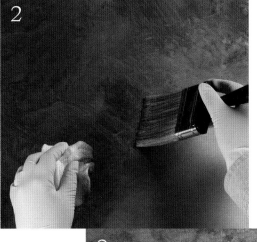

1 Basecoat the project surface with the gold paint.

2 Pour enough black paint into a paint pail to complete your surface. Add enough water to thin the paint to about whole milk consistency. Brush the black paint on and immediately pat with a cheesecloth wad.

3 While the black paint is still wet, dip the paintbrush 1" (2.5 cm) into the water; then selectively pounce areas on the piece. You are trying to puddle and pool the wet paint.

4 Soften the paint here and there by patting with a terry cloth rag. Take care to reveal areas of gold and deposits of black. If you remove too much paint, allow the surface to dry out and repeat the process.

5 Topcoat with one or two coats of varnish. The latex paint has been weakened by the addition of so much water and the topcoat will protect your beautiful work.

48 | Pickling

PICKLING IS ONE of a number of very old methods used to change the color of wood. The approach gives a very beautiful patina to any raw wood surface and is much less offensive than fuming, another color-altering technique.

Fuming is a process in which the vapors of a gas are used on woods that have natural tannin. Furniture makers have fumed wood for years. Charles Stickley of the Stickley furniture of the Arts and Craft period used the technique to achieve the beautiful colorations in his furniture.

The wood was placed in large fuming sheds and a (usually very secret) chemical combination was infused into the shed. Rather like a smokehouse for furniture!

Pickling, on the other hand, uses vinegar and steel wool. Putting the two together creates a chemical reaction that results in the solution used for pickling. It's easy to do, but be careful not to drip or spill the solution on your surface, as that will show.

Refer to pages 7, 8, and 14 before beginning.

MATERIALS AND TOOLS

- white distilled vinegar
- two steel wool pads, coarse
- paint pail
- sandpaper, 220-grit
- flat latex paintbrush, 3" (7.6 cm)

1 Soak the steel wool pads for 36 hours in ½ gallon (2 L) of white distilled vinegar.

2 Sand the raw wood smooth, lightly tack, then apply the vinegar mixture with the paintbrush and let nature take its course. The color develops fully after 24 hours. You may apply one or more coats to reach the depth of color you like.
Tip: Experiment in an inconspicuous place such as the inside of a drawer to see what color develops.

3 Topcoat with one or two coats of varnish or wax.
Note: The pine chair shown has had one pickling application and received a slight grayish discoloration. The top of the table and the drawer received a double application of the vinegar solution. Both of these pine pieces were new, raw wood, and are now softly altered. The insert shows pickling on an oak-veneered board. Veneer is thin and the solution stained the wood quickly and deeply into a dark gray.

TROMPE L'OEIL MEANS "the eye deceived" in French. Just as those who see this will be surprised it's not real, you will be surprised at how easily this technique allows you to render a believable raised panel.

Part of the art of trompe l'oeil is the manipulation of lights and darks to produce the shading that creates three-dimensionality on a two-dimensional surface.

The most important consideration is the direction from which your light source comes. This light source remains consistent and will be your "map" for placement of light and darks. For ease of rendering, keep it simple, select a two o'clock or ten o'clock direction. A two o'clock light source was used here.

49 | Trompe L'oeil Panel

Other factors for success concern the shading colors. If you apply a finish over the basecoat, you will need to complete the finish to judge the *overall* color before choosing shading colors. Use a version of the overall surface color that is about 60 percent darker for the dark shading. Use a lighter version about 50 percent lighter for the light shading.

You may use one or more of the techniques outlined in *50 Ways to Paint Furniture* to finish your project piece. The desk front shown is *Parchment* (page 68), the top is *Marble* (page 82), and the center is *Burled Wood* (page 86). Choosing the finish to use is part of the fun.

Refer to pages 7, 8, and 14 before beginning.

MATERIALS AND TOOLS

- flat latex paint for base, any color
- ruler
- pencil
- blue painter's tape, 1" (2.5 cm)
- flat latex paint, linen white
- flat latex paintbrush, 1" (2.5 cm)
- hair dryer
- flat latex paint for dark shade
- flat latex paint for light shade
- aluminum foil
- flat latex paint, black
- flat artist's latex paintbrush, ½" (1.3 cm)

1 Basecoat the project surface using your chosen colors and techniques.

2 Create the coved border for the panel by using the ruler and pencil to draw the outside edge of a rectangle. Adhere the tape along the inside of all of the lines. Place additional tape along the outside and inside edges of the first tape (like making a tape sandwich). Remove the first tape, creating a 1" (2.5 cm) panel border. Paint the panel border linen white using the latex paintbrush.

3 Place a piece of tape at a 45 degree angle on both corners of a section of the border (to create a crisp bevel). This tape will be moved to create bevels on each edge of the border. Work one section at a time to create the shadow illusion. Force-dry the paint with a hair dryer to move from section to section. Do not remove the panel border tapes until all the steps have been completed.

4 Double-load the latex paintbrush by loading one edge with the dark shading color and the other edge with the light shading color. Stroke the paintbrush on the aluminum foil to soften the colors and make them blend slightly in the center of the paintbrush.

Center the paintbrush on a border section, making sure the dark side of the paintbrush is in the appropriate place, and pull the paintbrush along the section. Do not worry if you have to re-load and go over it a

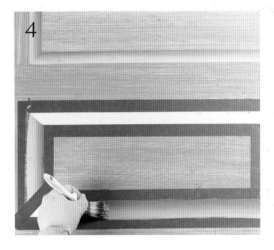

Continued on page 126

few times, as you want this paint to appear blended and soft. Allow to dry; then remove the corner bevel tape. Repeat the taping and painting until all the border sections have been completed.

Place the dark shade toward the center panel when painting the left and the bottom sections. Place the dark shade toward the outside when painting the right and the top sections. **Note:** The top of the first image shows what this step would look like if you pulled the tape at this point (but leave it in place).

5 Place a section of tape at the upper left and the lower right corners along the right side of the bevels. Mix a lowlight color using three-parts black and one-part dark shading color; thin it to whole milk consistency with water. Load one edge of the artist's paintbrush with lowlight color; blend it on the aluminum foil to soften. The paint should extend no farther than ¼" (6 mm) across the bristles. Place the color edge of the paintbrush on top of the dark shade color and pull across both sections. Allow to dry; then remove the corner tapes.

6 Shift the corner tapes to the left side of the bevels. Load the artist's paintbrush on one edge with white; blend it on the aluminum foil to soften. The paint should extend no farther than ¼" (6 mm) across the bristles. Place the color edge of the paintbrush on top of the lighter shade color and pull across both sections. Allow to dry, then remove the corner tapes.

7 Topcoat with one or two coats of varnish.

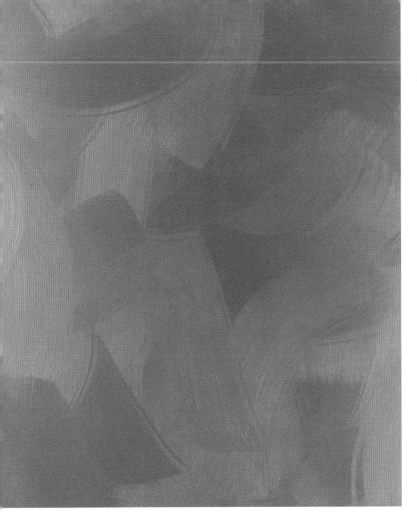

50 Burnished Metal

BURNISHED METAL OFFERS a subtle, pretty finish reminiscent of swirl-burnished sheet metal. It's suitable for furniture with contemporary lines. The finish is strong, durable, and very easy to touch up—plus, all metallic paints work with it.

Metallic paints are notorious for having an uneven appearance, owing, in great part, to their reflectivity. Purposefully adding movement with brushwork, as this finish does, allows light to dance off the surface, producing interest and playfulness.

Refer to *French Brush* (page 19) and pages 7 and 8 before beginning.

MATERIALS AND TOOLS

- latex paint, Modern Masters® Champagne (opaque) ME 206
- angle-edged latex paintbrush, 3" (7.6 cm)

1 Apply the metallic paint using the French brush technique. Allow the paint to dry, about one hour.

2 Repeat step 1.

3 Topcoat with one or two coats of varnish.

Author Biography

ELISE KINKEAD is an expert decorative painter specializing in the art of painted finishes for furniture and decoration. She has worked for select clients all over the country and also designs wall coverings. Her work has been published in local, regional, and national magazines and she is the co-author of *Mastering Fine Decorative Paint Techniques.*

Besides loving furniture as a canvas, she enjoys sharing her knowledge with others so that they may realize the delight in creating an object of beauty by challenging their artist within—both for self satisfaction and for the enjoyment of those who view the furniture.